Other Worlds Than This

Other Worlds Than This

Translations by
RACHEL HADAS

RUTGERS UNIVERSITY PRESS
New Brunswick, New Jersey

Publisher's Credits

Library of Congress Cataloging-in-Publication Data

Hadas, Rachel

Other worlds than this : translations / Rachel Hadas.

p. cm.

Translations of Tibullus, Seneca, Victor Hugo, Baudelaire, Mallarmé, Rimbaud, LaForgue, Valéry, and Karyotakis.

ISBN 0-8135-2067-3 (cloth)—ISBN 0-8135-2068-1 (pbk.)

1. Poetry—Translations into English. I. Title.

PN6101.H28 1994

808.81—dc20 93-33530

CIP

British Cataloging-in-Publication information available

Tibullus Odes I.ii, I.vi, and I.x originally appeared in *Arion, A Journal of Humanities and the Classics*, 3d ser., 2.1 (Winter 1992), published at Boston University.

Baudelaire's "Voyage to Cythera" and "The Owls"; LaForgue's "Winter Sunset" and "A Flash over the Abyss"; and Valéry's "Pomegrantes" originally appeared in *Tennessee Quarterly* 1 (1994).

Baudelaire's "The Swan" originally appeared in *Pequod* 35 (1993).

Baudelaire's "The Voice" originally appeared in *The New York Review of Books* (February 1991). Copyright © NYREV, Inc. Reprinted with permission from *The New York Review of Books.*

Baudelaire's "Sonnet in Autumn," "Retreat," "Misty Sky," and "The Promises of a Face" appeared in *Raritan* 11, no. 1 (Summer 1991).

Rimbaud's "Ophelia"; Karyotakis's "How Young" and "Preveza" originally appeared in *Harvard Review* (Spring 1992).

Valéry's "Aurora" originally appeared in *PN Review* (1990).

In Loving Memory of

Moses Hadas
(1900-1966)

Elizabeth Chamberlayne Hadas
(1915-1992)

Lewis Parke Chamberlayne
(1879-1917)
and
Charles Andrew Barber
(1956-1992)

Acknowledgments

I offer this book to the memories of the four extraordinary people who either in their lives or from the far side of death helped these translations to come into being. My father, among many other things a versatile, fluent, and expert translator, was a constant source of energy and confidence. My mother, who patiently helped scores of girls including me to understand the intricacies of Latin poetry and to love all poetry, was the first person I ever knew who embodied a passion for literature. My grandfather, whose beautiful translations I encountered only after my mother's death, silently steered me between the clashing rocks of choices that all translators face, and convinced me from beyond the grave, as if I still needed further proof, that the love of translating must be an inherited trait. Finally, Charles Barber in the course of our short and joyful friendship quickly came to personify for me what he still represents: the attentive love of all the arts and the passionate receptivity as well as the "luxe, calme, et volupté" necessary for poetry to flourish.

I can thank and love the dead, as I can do my work, only because I am bolstered by the love of the living — George and Jonathan.

I want to thank Diane Rayor for giving me the opportunity to translate Tibullus; she and William Batstone edited my drafts with great learning and acuity. David Slavitt and Palmer Bovie gave me the opportunity to translate Seneca. James Merrill, whose superb rendering of Valéry's "Palme" has been for me a beacon of what translation can be, was a source of encouraging comments and helpful suggestions for revision. Roger Gobineau shed light on some obscure passages of Rimbaud. Ben Sonnenberg, alerted by an epigraph, first encouraged me to write about Karyotakis, and Edmund Keeley and Stratis Haviaras cheered on my attempts to translate him. Mostly, however, I have consulted no one; and I alone am responsible for all mistranslations.

Thanks are due to the Virginia Center for the Creative Arts, where some of these translations were done, and to the Faculty Academic Study Program of Rutgers University, which was generous with the twin resources of time and money in the fall term of 1992; to John Heuston for his word-processing skill and speed; to the entire staff of Rutgers University Press; and above all to the Director of the Press, Kenneth Arnold, who in his capacity as my editor continues to be an indefatigable source of wisdom and enthusiasm.

Contents

Introduction

I must have been in the eighth grade when I took pleasure in translating Verlaine's "L'Art Poétique" into rhymed quatrains. Later on, in college, I translated a bit of Tibullus and a speech from Sophocles' *Ajax* into indifferent iambics. In the 1970s, I translated a collection of poems by the Greek poet Stephanos Xenos and a lyrical essay by G.–A. Mangakis. Finally, my abortive attempt to translate Sylvia Plath's "Poppies in July" *into* Greek is the subject of my poem "A Copy of *Ariel*."

None of those translations is worth exhuming, let alone reprinting. It wasn't until the summer of 1989 that I had some success in translating a poem whose intricacy of form was matched by its shimmering elusiveness: Valéry's "Aurore." And another year went by before I tried my hand again. When, early in the summer of 1990, I began to translate some poems of Baudelaire, it wasn't a considered decision; I seem to have simply started. "Sonnet in Autumn" came first, followed by "The Fountain of Blood," and then, happy with both the process and the results, I pressed on, for the next two or three weeks, at the rate of a poem every couple of days.

Serendipitous as it sometimes felt, the act of putting these poems into English was nevertheless overdetermined. For one thing, Baudelaire had long been a crucial poet for me. My 1988 essay "The Cradle and the Bookcase" owes its title to the first line of "La Voix," a poem I didn't feel ready to translate at the time. As early as 1983, I had written a brief comparison of Baudelaire and Karyotakis, a poet who then seemed to me too intimidatingly elegant, idiosyncratic, and complex to be translatable at all. Indeed, as far as I know, I'm the first person to have attempted a translation of some poems of Karyotakis into English (this was to happen in 1991); whereas Baudelaire has of course been blessed and cursed with innumerable versions. Richard Howard's complete rendering of *Les Fleurs du Mal* (Godine, 1982), one of the most recent of these and arguably the best, was the book that first brought Baudelaire into focus for me.

Once I realized I was embarked on a project of translating, other kinds of forces came into play, such as requests to translate some elegies of Tibullus and a tragedy of Seneca. But no matter how pleasurable and instructive such tasks proved to be, they remained assignments rather than impulse—assignments which would never have been accepted without the unexpected intensity of my first experiences translating Baudelaire.

Aside from a conviction, as I settled down to work in June of 1990, that the poems in *Fleurs du Mal* could and should be made to rhyme in English, I had no conscious thought of improving on previous translations. I was doing this work for the pleasure of the repeated plunges it afforded into a seductive and alarming medium — not just an element, a world.

I was constantly aware, as I proceeded, of the poetry group I had been leading up through the previous month at Gay Men's Health Crisis in New York. Illness and sensuality, desire and despair, the bleak reality of a winter city and the dream of freedom and repose—such yokings had their counterparts in the lives and work I had encountered week by week all year. As I made my way via the first few poems into Baudelaire's peculiar territory, I kept thinking in particular of one of the writers in the group, Charles Barber, whom it is not too much to call the presiding Muse of the first crop of these translations. Nineteen-ninety was the first summer of Charles's and my friendship. I didn't know at the time that it was also our next-to-last summer; but the poems that pulled at me week after week knew more than I did. "You glow with beauty like an autumn sky,/But sadness rinses over me like water." "Overwhelming Night begins her reign,/Shady and damp and wafting unknown ills."

As always, summer in Vermont worked its magic. I'd look up from "Africa behind a wall of sleet" to gaze at the pine trees on the hill. My husband might be wandering past, or I might glimpse him sunning himself in a battered lawn chair, puffing on his pipe, working out visible (chess) or invisible problems in silence. My mother might cross my line of vision, trowel in hand, moving slowly. That was her next-to-last summer too.

By early August, when I had to go down to Newark on Rutgers business, I had translated twenty-one poems. I knew by this time that more would follow, and they did: more Baudelaire in 1991, as well as various poems by Rimbaud, Valéry, Mallarmé, and Karyotakis, followed by the Tibullus selections and Seneca's *Oedipus;* in 1992 a few more poems by Baudelaire, and the LaForgue and Hugo selections.

But now it was time to take a break. The night train back from Newark to Montpelier turned out to provide an ideal capsule in which to reflect and remember. By dawn, my meandering thoughts had just about reached the point of equating the time and space on the train with the process of translation itself. Stanzas, for example, seemed to me to resemble roomettes such as the one I was in, boxes designed in advance, compartments for a train trip that might get one where one wanted to go but whose itinerary was not of one's own devising.

Translating Baudelaire during the previous weeks had felt to me like a bold, impulsive act. Yet at the same time, something about the spaces in his work provoked extreme caution. Rash as I had been to encroach at all, I had entered each stanza, no, every line of each stanza of those twenty-one poems as a careful servant would enter a room, polishing facets, highlighting ornaments without displacing any important documents, restoring its primal luster to all the crucial and artful original disorder. The surface of each separate syllable gleamed as I gingerly advanced.

I thought of red and black lacquer, of an ebony box on a mahogany table, of an inlaid dagger in a lamplit corner.

Each unit presented its own riddle. Each was a problem I could solve without shattering it only if I moved gently, brushing the faintest layer of the dust of disuse from the arc of an alexandrine or shifting an unintelligible object (love gift? souvenir?) a shade closer to the reddish glow of firelight, while twilight filled the room and in the hearth the dying embers faintly whistled.

Not that Baudelaire's world was wholly denuded of daylight. He had his sunny afternoons and misty, rainy mornings. But still, in this predominantly wintry world the essential hallmark was that indoor phenomenon the room—the stanza. Even to ponder the act of translation moved my mind inexorably indoors. To attempt a translation, after all, meant to step from one world to another—from nature to the artificer's workshop. Nabokov compared the project of translating Shakespeare to the paradoxical undertaking of constructing a kind of robot tree in order to replicate, not the original tree, but its effects.

> It was as if someone, having seen a certain oak tree (further called Individual T) growing in a certain land and casting its own unique shadow on the green and brown ground, had proceeded to erect in his garden a prodigiously intricate piece of machinery which was as unlike that or any other tree as the translator's inspiration and language were unlike those of the original author, but which, by means of ingenious combinations of parts, light effects, breeze-engendering engines, would when

> completed, cast a shadow exactly similar to that of Individual T—the same outline, changing in the same manner, with the same double and single spots of suns rippling in the same position, at the same hour of the day. From a practical point of view, such a waste of time and material (those headaches, those midnight triumphs that turn out to be disasters in the sober light of the morning!) was almost criminally absurd, since the greatest masterpiece of imitation presupposed a voluntary limitation of thought, in submission to another man's genius. *(Bend Sinister)*

My first thought on reading that passage was that the translator, "midnight triumphs" and all, was a mad scientist figure, galvanizing something lifeless into a semblance of animation. But this facile analogy gave way, as soon as I started translating Baudelaire, to respect and compassion at the monumental selflessness required by such an undertaking. The question Nabokov went on to ponder was whether "this suicidal limitation and submission [could] be compensated by the miracle of adaptive tactics, by the thousand devices of shadography, by the keen pleasure that the weaver of words and their witness experienced at every new wile in the warp." Clearly, for the translator of Pushkin's *Onegin* the pleasure did indeed compensate for the tribulation.

And when all I'd done was inhabit and cautiously tidy a dark red velvet roomette for a short and wholly voluntary journey, how could I not agree? For the pleasure of wandering out of doors I had briefly substituted the more circumscribed pleasure of these zip-up curtains, this wet dawn framed by thick windows, this temporary confinement with its illusion of invulnerability. Had it really been such a sacrifice?

"Hardly anything," Freud writes, "is harder to give up than a pleasure which we have once experienced. Actually, we can never give anything up; we only exchange one idea for another." What I had been doing in working on Baudelaire was exchanging one kind of challenge, one kind of exploration, for another. The process wasn't always delicious. Folded tightly into the prearranged dimensions of the roomette, or tinkering with the robot tree, I sometimes felt tucked too snugly into the bed of the poem. The thought of a tidy bed, as I lay half-awake in my berth, stirred the memory of a dream a few months old, a dream that as surely as the strong arms of a nurse had shifted me from the vertical to the horizontal. In the dream I had seemed to sink down and back into a low seat like Chester Kallman's killer armchair in the final year of his life. It was comfortable, indeed luxurious, this seat — far too engulfingly soft to consider getting up from. So there I was, settling (the dream informed me) into a world of illness. For this turned out to be a hospital room I was sharing with Charlie, the real friend whose dream kiss of welcome conveyed affection and infection in equal doses. Parallel beds: having become equals in the dream (for I was lying down by now), we'd wait it out together.

To the memory of this dream was added that of Vaclav Havel's last prison letter to his wife, in which he wrote that people are nailed down to a grid of paradoxes, stretched (it sounds like torture) between the world's horizontal and the vertical of Being. Could this be why people struck poses of such curious distortion? Our metaphysical dilemma was a gift to chiropractors. I thought of how people stood or walked, listing or twisted from invisible weights. Of how my own mind moved in an incorrigible zigzag, a sidestep like a dancing dog's across dark gaps where, as barbaric cages once ordained, one could neither lie nor stand nor sit. Were these dark gaps our places for the duration of the journey?

In the hospital dream, my ungrantable wish was to save my friend as best I could by sharing his illness— sharing, where salvation is impossible, being the next best thing. Short of actually curing Charlie, I tried to become him, to translate myself into his situation. But in the long run, and out of the realm of dreams, translating him and the others into Baudelaire, or vice versa—the "matelas d'épingles" into "a thicket of IVs"—proved, though still impotent, the better way of combating mortality.

The sun was coming out. My train of thought, transformed into a means of locomotion, was pulling into Montpelier Junction. Already I was scrambling out of my compartment, that tiny hutch that had housed me for twelve hours or so. How small, stale, and cramped it would seem (or would it?) if I looked back! The conductor was unfolding the step. Down on the platform my husband and son were standing, George waving, Jonathan beaming. An interlude of real life was about to resume, requiring a form of love simpler, maybe, but no less elusive than the process of transformation I had been engaged in. I could accommodate both; I had to. My notebook stowed in my shoulderbag, I climbed down the steep little stairs.

TIBULLUS
(48–19 BCE)

Tibullus I.i (*"Divitias alius . . ."*)

Let someone else heap wealth up in a pile
Of gold, and own vast acres of rich soil.
When enemies approach, he's terrified;
The trumpets blare and sleep deserts his bed.
Let peaceful poverty be my tranquil lot,
The home-fires always glowing in the grate.

When planting season rolled around, I'd graft
Young vines and apples with a rustic craft.
Bountiful Hope would yield a bumper crop,
Filling every vessel to the top,
For lonely stumps can be my prayers' abode,
Or flower-decked stones that mark a triple road.
Whatever first-fruits harvest season yields,
I offer to the patron god of fields.

Ceres, let a crown of homegrown wheat
Hang up to decorate your temple gate.
And in the garden let Priapus stand
To frighten birds, his sickle in his hand.
You Lares, patrons of a property
That prospered once, accept your gift from me:
A slaughtered heifer once upon a time,
But now the farm yields only one small lamb
To grace the feast at which the country boys
Pray for "Good crops! Good wine!" with joyful noise.

If only I could make my home right here
And not keep moving on forevermore,
I'd seek out shade, the Dog-star rising high,
Under a tree, some burbling brook nearby.
I wouldn't be too proud to wield a spade
Or urge on lazy oxen with a goad:
Any abandoned kid or little lamb
Left by its mother I would carry home.

Robbers and wolves, please spare my little flock;
Do your plundering from some richer stock.
Of flock and shepherd both I take good care—
Lustrations and libations every year.
O gods, be present at my humble feast!
My simple crockery is clean, at least.
(A farmer first invented pottery,
Molding drinking cups from the soft clay.)

My father's fortune, grandfather's rich crop,
Carefully garnered—these I can give up;
A humble income is enough for me,
And a bed to sleep in peacefully.
Delicious, hearing the wild wind's alarms
While cuddled up within my mistress's arms,
And when harsh gales drench all the world in mire,
To sit and snooze in safety by the fire!
So much for me; all riches I resign
To those who can put up with wind and rain.

Let all gold rot, and every emerald too,
Rather than one girl weep to see us go!
Messalla, over land and sea you roam,
To hang your wartime trophies up at home;
While by a woman's beauty fettered here,
Janitorlike I guard her stubborn door.

What I want, Delia, isn't praise but you—
Let them call me sluggish, lazy too.
You I will gaze at in my dying hour,
You I will touch with my hand's failing power.
And when upon the funeral pyre I lie,
Your tears and kisses will gush forth for me.
You'll weep because your heart is not of brass;
Your tender bosom hides no flinty place.
From my funeral no one will go home
Dry-eyed, neither maiden nor young man.
But Delia, no melodrama, please.
Hair-tearing or cheek-scratching—omit these.

All this will come. Turn now to love instead,
Before dark Death sneaks up with muffled head
And feeble Age limps forward. It's not right
To say sweet nothings when your hair is white.
Under indulgent Venus' auspices,
We now can be as riotous as we please.
Here I command the troops—and order them
To turn their weapons against jealous men
Who prosper—fine! My livelihood's secure;
I can look down on both the rich and poor.

Tibullus I.ii ("*Adde merum vinoque . . .*")

Fill up my glass again! The anodyne
For this poor lover's pain is sleep—and wine.
And when I've swilled enough to sink a ship,
No busybody better wake me up.
A cruel door stands between my girl and me,
Double-locked with a determined key.

Damn you, door! May rainstorms mildew you,
Or well-aimed lightning burn you through and through.
Aren't you moved by all my misery?
Please, door, open just a crack for me,
But carefully—don't creak. If I just said
Harsh things, may curses light on my own head.
I hope you've not forgotten all my prayers,
And all the times I hung your knob with flowers.

You, Delia, must be bold and cunning too;
Venus helps those who help themselves, you know.
Whether a boy sneaks to a strange room or
Stealthily a girl unlocks the door,
Venus teaches sorties out of bed,
Teaches our footsteps soundlessly to pad,
Or lovers to communicate by sighs
Before the hoodwinked husband's very eyes.
But you must have initiative, and dare
To prowl around at midnight without fear.

Take me—I wander through the streets all night.
Plenty of thieves and muggers are in sight,
But Love protects me from the switchblade knife
Scenario ("Your money or your life!").
In holiness a lover's safety lies;
It's needless to envision plots and spies.
No frosty winter night can do me harm;
Rain falls in torrents, but I'm safe and warm.
True, now I'm suffering; that could turn around
If Delia beckoned me without a sound.

Whoever sees us, please pretend you didn't;
Venus prefers her lovers snugly hidden.
Don't make a racket, do not ask my name
Or blind me with an outthrust torch's flame.
If you were fool enough to see us, then
Pray to the gods that you'll forget again.
The tattletale must learn the parentage
(Tempest and blood) that fuels Venus' rage.

But even if some busybody tells
Your husband all about us, magic spells
Will seal his eyes. A witch has promised me.
I've seen her pull the stars down from the sky.
Her charms can change a running river's flow,
Split open graves and let dead spirits go.
From pyres still smoldering she can wheedle bones,
Commanding ghostly troops with weird groans;
Then, sprinkling milk, she orders them away.
Clouds she disperses from a sullen sky.

In midsummer she can make it snow;
She knows Medea's herbs and where they grow;
The hounds of Hecate she can tame at will.

To cheat him, she's concocted me a spell
To chant three times, and each time spit as well.
From that time on, no matter what he sees,
He'll be unable to believe his eyes.
But keep away from other men! He'll be
Suspicious of every man but me.
This sorceress claimed that she could cure me too;
Her charms and herbs could set me free—of you.
She purified me at the witching hour
By torchlight, and slew victims with her power.
But what I prayed for was a love to share;
Life without you would be bleak and bare.

Ironheaded fool, who had you in his bed
But chose a military life instead!
Let him parade his troops of prisoners forth
And pitch his tent on bloody captured earth.
His armor's silver worked with gold, of course,
So let him preen in it astride his horse.
For myself, let me yoke up my two
Oxen and plow, so long as I'm with you.
When we are intertwined in one embrace,
Sweet sleep on the bare ground is no disgrace.
Why toss on purple counterpanes, awake

And weeping all night for a lost love's sake?
Down comforters, rich bedspreads cannot bring
Sleep, nor can soft water murmuring.

Have I offended with my blasphemy,
Venus, and do I pay the penalty?
Can it be said that I've profaned the shrine,
Despoiled the altar of its boughs divine?
If this were true I'd go down on all fours
And plant a kiss upon the temple floor;
Kneeling in supplication on the ground,
Against the door my wretched head I'd pound.

Whoever finds this laughable—you'll see!
You too will suffer from Love's cruelty.
An oldster thinks a lovelorn youth's a joke,
But soon his wrinkled neck is in the yoke.
He whistles senile ditties to the air
And carefully arranges his white hair,
Loiters for hours at his beloved's gate
And buttonholes her servant in the street.
Children pursue him, a malicious flock
Who spit in their own bosoms for good luck.

Venus, I've always served you faithfully.
Don't burn your harvest in your rage at me!

Tibullus I.vi ("*Semper, ut inducar . . .*")

Cheerfully smiling, Love, at first you come
To draw me in; but once I'm caught you're glum,
Sullen, and savage. Is it worth your while
To have entrapped a mortal by your guile?

Spread out your snares, now Delia secretly
At blackest midnight kisses—well, not me.
A fig for all her fervid protestations
Of innocence!—familiar proclamations
To my ear, for it isn't long since she
Made them to her husband about me.
Yes, I was fool enough to teach her how
To play the tricks whose victim I am now,
Like cooking up a need for privacy
At bedtime, and then tiptoeing to me,
Or using herbal remedies to smooth
The telltale blemishes left by Love's tooth.

And you, dimwitted spouse of this deceiver,
Take it from me: you never should believe her.
A friendly gossip session may appear
Harmless, or a dress cut down to here—
Watch out! She'll dip her finger in a cup,
Trace assignations on the table top.
Or she'll develop endless rendezvous
At women's rites—men, these are not for you.
I'd follow, if you left it up to me,
Straight to the altar. Trust what you can see.

Pretending to admire her wedding band,
I often found a way to touch her hand;

I'd send you off to sleep with wine while I
Watered my own and drank adultery.
Pardon me, please; I never meant to harm you.
Love forced me to it, and such gods disarm you.
I am he—discretion, now take flight!—
The man your dog was barking at all night.
Why have her, when you treat her carelessly?
The door is shut, but you forgot the key.

In bed she's breathing hard—for other men;
Then suddenly that migraine's back again.
Leave her to me. I wouldn't mind the whip;
Cheerfully I'd let them chain me up.
Away, all you who preen for hours on end,
Languorous togas flowing to the ground.
Whoever sees us, keep your conscience free;
Cross the street or look the other way.

All this is by arrangement of a god,
Or so a priestess prophesied out loud,
Who when the war-god whirls across her mind
Leaves fear of fire and torture far behind,
Cuts her own flesh, and doesn't hesitate
To rinse an idol in the scarlet spate,
And having pierced herself right through the chest
Chants oracles, blood flowing from her breast:
"Since Love is this girl's guardian, treat her well;
Who touches her will suffer from my spell.
As blood from me, so shall his money flow
Away and vanish, dust to winds that blow."

Some punishment she also meted out,
Delia, to you. I pray that it be slight.
Not on your account, you understand;

Your good old mother stays my angry hand.
Trembling in darkness she leads you to me
And joins our hands in silence, secretly.
My footsteps sing an individual song
To her who's waited by the door so long.

Long life to you, old woman! And I'd give
You, if I could, some of my years to live.
Because of you I'll always love your daughter;
You know the saying about blood and water.
But though a matron's gown is out of place,
Do teach her to be faithful nonetheless.
I too will be all virtue. If I praise
Another girl, she may scratch out my eyes,
And if I cheat her, drag me by the hair
Upside down right through the public square.

Sooner than ever lift a hand to you,
I'd have it cut off—and the other too.
Let it be not fear but fidelity
That in my absence keeps you true to me.
The girl who's true to no one in old age
Turns to a crone who's weaving for a wage,
Guiding her wool through someone else's loom,
Working her shaky fingers to the bone.
The young men laugh at this pathetic sight
And all agree it serves the old bag right.
From high Olympus Venus too beholds her:
"See the rewards of sluttishness!" she scolds her.

Let whom the shoe fits wear it, Delia. We
Will be a model couple till we die.

Tibullus I.x ("*Quis fuit horrendos . . .*")

Whoever first invented swords was more
Than merely fierce, but feral to the core!
First battles and then warfare, genocide—
A whole new way to death he opened wide.

Poor devil, can we blame him in the least?
We make ill use of weapons meant for beasts.

I lay the blame at riches' gilded door.
People used beechen cups in times of yore.
Safely flocks wandered, and when day was done
Among his ewes the lordly ram lay down.

Had I lived then, I never would have known
Weapons, or shuddered hearing trumpets blown.
But now I'm dragged to war. Some enemy
Already wields the sword that will slay me.

Save me, you household gods! Remember, it
Is I, the child who frolicked at your feet.
Even a carved log can be put to use;
You're the ancestral guardians of our house.
Religion meant more when a humble shrine
Sheltered a god small, wooden, but divine,
Who favored any man who brought him fruit
Or bound his carven head with ears of wheat.
Prayers satisfied, whole families would bring
Wheatcakes and honey as an offering.

You Lares, ward off weapons from us; I
Promise you a hog fresh from the sty.
I'll follow, robed in white from head to toe,
My temples wreathed in myrtle as I go.
But let it be another man who (Mars
Aiding him) is triumphant in the wars
And tells me every last exploit again,
Sketching the troops' position out in wine.

Insanity, pursuing Death this way!
Soon enough she approaches stealthily
To take us to the land where nothing grows,
But Cerberus barks and horrid Charon rows
Across the Styx forever. Throngs of souls
Pallid and ashen-faced drift past dim pools.

Leave that. The patriarch whose family
Surrounds his ripe age—that's the man for me!
He is a shepherd, his son tends the lambs;
His wife heats water for their weary limbs.
May I thus, tranquil, hair as white as snow,
Tell stories of what I did long ago.

May radiant Peace, who first taught bulls to plow,
Cultivate our fruitful acres now.
Peace pressed the juices from the swollen vine
So sons inherit the paternal wine.
In peacetime hoe and plow gleam, free of rust,
While neglected weapons gather dust.

Homeward wends the farmer (he's none too
Sober) with his family in row.
Then Venus' war heats up. The woman's hair
Is torn, cheeks scratched; he's beaten down the door.
She weeps; but he, victorious, weeps too
To think of all the damage he can do.
Love plants himself between the angry pair
And mischievously makes their quarrel flare.

A man who strikes his girl is iron, is stone;
He drags the gods down from their heavenly throne.
Sufficient if he peels her thin dress off her,
Sufficient if he musses up her coiffure
And makes her cry. What blessings that man bears
Who can move a tender girl to tears!
But nothing rough—or let him take his shield
And march himself right out of Venus' field.

Come, fostering Peace, the harvest fruits bestowing,
A cornucopia filled to overflowing.

SENECA (4–65 CE)

Selections from *The Tragedy of Oedipus*

[Scene 1]

OEDIPUS

Rising resignedly through smears of gray,
the sun slinks back to drive the dark away.
To houses stricken with this ravenous plague
it brings a lurid light:
each dawn uncovers wreckage from last night.

Who would want to be a king, I ask—
horrors heaped behind a grinning mask!
Rocks that jut out into the open sea
are drubbed by breakers on the quietest day,
vulnerable and naked as a king
daily exposed to every passing thing.

I shunned the sceptre that my sire would leave me.
Exiled and bold, without a care to grieve me,
I wandered; and—I swear it by the sky!—
blindly stumbled into royalty.
O God, unspeakable the things I fear—
by my own hand somehow to kill my sire,
or so the Delphic oracle gives out.
And something even worse is hinted at
than murdering my father—some vile curse

too foul to speak of. Phoebus in my eyes
flashes the bed where my own father lies!
This threatening image made me leave the place.
My life at home was innocent, I say;
my effort was forever to obey
the laws of Nature. But when what you fear
is so enormous, though it may appear
impossible, you shudder all the time:
Can I, could I commit this dreadful crime?
Yes, Fate's concocting something just for me,
now, now this instant!
How can this not be
when right and left my kinsmen are mown down?
Some special hell's reserved for me alone.
The city crumbles—fodder fresh at hand
for Death's forever hungry maw. I stand
safe and sound as far as I can see,
but still a doomed man, still Apollo's prey,
marked by the aura of foreboding fate:
the very life I've lived pollutes the state.

We burn with fever, but no breezes cool
our faces, and the August sun adds fuel
to feed the summer's flames. The streams dry up
and the thin grass grows colorless with drought.
Dirce's depleted, Ismenus so low
that through its sluggish waters bare banks show.
Down a dark sky the sun's pale sister slinks;
daylight dwindles to a feeble wink.
Even on clear nights, no stars appear;
a black miasma shrouds the atmosphere.

Heaven's happy houses, palaces of gods,
look dim, diminished. Grain within the pod
nods its golden top, then dries and dies.

No group's immune from such calamities:
all ages and both sexes are cut down.
The dreadful plague joins babies and old men,
parents and children. A shared funeral pyre
is common: for each family, one fire.
Few are the survivors left to mourn;
most of them are ash within the urn.
All funeral rites now are abbreviated.
Who's left to weep? The city's decimated.
The monstrousness of what's befallen us
keeps us from weeping. Tears are little use
when a bewildered father lifts his son
onto the pyre. The mother, crazed, brings one,
then scurries back again to fetch another
for the same flames that just consumed his brother.
Lamentations may be at their height;
they're interrupted as fresh griefs break out.
Pyres people have reserved for their own use
are loaded with another family's corpse.
Fire is precious now, so people steal it.
Shame? In our wretchedness we do not feel it.
We lack the graves to cover up the bones.
Fire is sufficient—yet it hardly burns
more than a fraction truly through and through.
Earth is lacking, timber's lacking too
for mounds and pyres. And no prayer or skill
can help the sick; the healers too fall ill.

*　　*　　*

[Creon describes the summoning of shades.]

CREON

A somber grove of trees stands far from town
near Dirce's valley; rivulets run down.
One cypress, loftiest in all that place,
clasps the whole forest in its green embrace;
like open arms an ancient oak holds out
its great curved branches, riddled now with rot.
Huge chunks of one long years have nibbled at;
another's crooked, split clear to the root.
In this place bitter-berried laurels grow,
and slender linden trees, and myrtle too;
alders whose timber sails the seven seas
and knotty pine exposed to every breeze.
Amidst all these trees, an enormous one
shades the smaller saplings from the sun.
Its giant branches, spreading far and wide,
furnish a kind of fort for all the wood.
Beneath this tree, untouched by light of day,
an icy river wends its sluggish way.
Spongy swamps are everywhere about.
When the old priest approached this gloomy spot
forever veiled in its peculiar night,
a ditch was swiftly dug, and glowing coals
flung into it (snatched first from funerals).
The priest, now garbed in a funereal gown,
takes a branch and waves it up and down.
Cloaked in deep mourning, the old man moves on;

his inky robes are trailing on the ground,
his white hair tied with sprigs of deadly yew.
Black-fleeced sheep and oxen of dark hue
are dragged away. The fed flames leap and thrive
as in their ghastly fire the victims writhe.
Dead spirits and their king the priest invokes
first, then the keeper of Lake Lethe's lock,
chants magic spells; and, foaming at the mouth,
repeats a charm that has the power to soothe
or to compel the shades that flit about.
Next upon the altar he pours out
blood; burns whole victims; fills the trench with gore.
Then a stream of snowy milk he pours
and, with his left hand, wine; and calls again
upon the spirits in a wilder tone.

Hecate's hounds were howling, and the sound
three times made the whole valley floor resound.
"They hear me!" cries the priest. "What I have said
has burst blind Chaos and released the dead."
The whole wood cringed; its leaves stood up like hair.
Stout oaks split open, forests quaked with fear,
the earth shrank back and gave a dreadful groan.
Indignant at this breach of Acheron
or else travailing to give passage to
the dead, she shrieked, all barriers burst through!
Or triple Cerberus it might have been,
angrily worrying his massive chain.
Then earth yawned. An enormous gulf spread wide.
And I beheld the shadowy pools inside,
and pallid gods of quintessential night.
My thick blood clotted in my veins with fright

as troops of savage creatures leaped out, stood
in arms before me—that whole snaky brood
of brothers sprung once from the dragon's teeth.
Then grim Erinys and blind Fury shrieked,
and Horror, and whatever teeming forms
in such eternal darkness breed by swarms—
hair-tearing Grief, and Sickness, her poor head
scarcely upright; Old Age, and looming Dread;
and hungry Plague who gobbles nations up.
At such a spectacle, our spirits stop.
Even the girl, who from her father knew
such necromancy, was astonished too.
But her undaunted sire Tiresias
summoned the bloodless throng of ghosts to us.
Like clouds they float, and drink in the fresh air.
More than the leaves of autumn whirling down,
more than spring flowers massed in fullest bloom
among which a great globe of bees appears,
more than the waves that wash Ionian shores,
more than the birds that, fleeing winter chills,
crisscross the skies, exchanging snow for Nile's
warm waters—far more numerous than all
these were the ghosts responsive to his call.
Trembling, they flock where shade is to be found.
Zethus first emerges from the ground,
clutching a fierce bull by the horns. And then,
a lyre in his left hand, comes Amphion,
the sweetness of whose melodies split stone.
Then Niobe, safe now among her sons,
with haughty gaze re-counts her ghostly brood;
then Agave, a far worse mother, mad
and raving still. Along with her she brings
the Maenad troops who tore apart the king.

And mutilated Pentheus follows them,
still furiously angry, threatening doom.
Repeatedly called forth, a certain shade
far from the others lifts his guilty head
and tries to hide. The priest renews his pleas
and finally we glimpse the hidden face—
Laius! I shudder at the very sound.
The sight was fearful: blood was all around,
his filthy hair was matted in a mass.
He raged at us:

"O Cadmus' horrid house,
ever rejoicing to shed kindred blood,
brandish your thyrsus, savage your own brood
sooner than commit what is the true
desire of every man in Thebes to do—
sleep with his mother! Not heavenly wrath, my town,
no, nothing but your own crimes drags you down!
You suffer—not from stormwinds from the south,
nor from earth parched by a destructive drought,
but from your king, who bought his reign with blood
and occupies the bed his father should—
appalling offspring of the monstrous womb
that bore him first, then swelled again by him.
Returning to the source from which he'd come,
he did a deed that even wild beasts shun,
himself begetting brothers of his own—
a knottier tangle than the Sphinx by far!
You wield that blood-stained sceptre; I, your sire,
still unavenged, will haunt you everywhere.
Fury as bridesmaid keeps me company—
her hissing whiplash cracks resoundingly.
Your whole incestuous household I'll lay low,
plotting violence for its overthrow.

So take your king and fling him far from here,
an exile, to whatever land can bear
his poisoned presence. Once he leaves this place,
it will recapture springtime's verdant grace,
lifegiving air we'll once again breathe deep
as in the forests beauty wakes from sleep.
Plague, death, destruction, labor, waste, and pain,
exiled with him, will never come again.
And even as he hastens to find ways
of quick escaping, I'll concoct delays.
With nothing but a staff to guide each step,
a wavering path of blackness he shall grope.
You Theban elders, exile is for you
to force on him; I'll darken his sky too."

* * *

[The Messenger's Speech]

MESSENGER

Once Oedipus perceived the whole foul dread
that was his birthright, onto his own head
he showered curses, and with hurrying feet
sped to the palace, mulling on his fate.
A savage lion on the Libyan plain
rages and roars and tosses its gold mane;
so, wild of eye, distorted by his passion,
he groaned—no, howled. An icy perspiration
covered his body, as a foaming tide

of long quiescent sorrows overflowed.
Some appalling stroke is in his mind
to match his fate—and bring it to an end.
"Why am I waiting? Why delay?" he moans.
"Stab me, someone! Shatter me with stones,
or let a fire consume my sins to ash!
Tigers and vultures, batten on my flesh!
Accursed Cithaeron, lair of nothing good,
send out wild beasts against me from your wood,
set a pack of slavering hounds on me
or the ferocious queen, mad Agave!
My soul, death's nothing fearful, no offense;
death preserves the good man's innocence."

These were his words. He drew his sword, and then:

"Is this the way? Such dreadful crimes with one
blow to be dissolved, the penalty
forever paid? Yes, for your father die—
punishment enough for that. But not
for her who bore you, on whom you begot
an evil breed of offspring—not for her!
If you're the sinner, she's the sufferer,
utterly ruined. And your country bleeds!
Suicide can't atone for these misdeeds.
No; let that nature which, in fashioning me,
forsook her laws and standards utterly,
transform herself once more on my behalf
to punish me with freakish shapes of wrath.
Let me live a brand-new life, then die,

only to be reborn to misery,
a never-ending cycle. This takes thought:
some unique form of punishment stretched out,
some death continual, lingering; some way
where, shunned by live and dead alike, I'll stray
toward slow extinction, not a sudden end.
How can you shrink from such a sentence, friend?"

Sobs like a sudden rainstorm wet his face.

"Weeping is useless, tears a mere disgrace.
Ah, but if my eyes themselves I scrape
out of their sockets, then—like tears in shape—
they can rain down. Gods of connubial night,
let this be your sacrifice: my sight!"

These were his words. Cheeks blazing fiery red,
delirious, eyes starting from his head,
of desperation's violent power full,
he groaned. His fingers clawed into his skull.
His eyes wait, avid, ready for his hands,
and rush to meet them, eager for the wound.
His nails rake out all lingering shreds of light,
ripping loose the very roots of sight.
All blind and empty! Still, his hand's employed
scraping the hollow, picking at the void.
His maddened ravings too go on and on,
but somehow their immediacy is gone.
Now that he is finally free of sight,

he lifts his head to catch a glimpse of night.
Scanning the heavens with his empty eyes,
he rips away a lingering ribbon, cries
to all the gods triumphantly: "I pray
you, spare Thebes now! I've paid the penalty;
I've found a sure way to make old wrongs right.
My dark past matches this unending night."

Now from his mangled face a shower of gore
bursts out afresh, blood spraying everywhere.

VICTOR HUGO
(1802–1885)

At Dawn Tomorrow

I know that you are waiting, and tomorrow I shall go;
At dawn tomorrow, at the hour the fields begin to glow.
I'll follow all the forest paths, I'll go the mountain way.
Apart from you I can no longer stay.

I'll walk along and look at nothing but what's in my head,
Hear nothing either, and see nothing else on either side,
Alone, unknown, arms folded, bowed down by a heavy
  weight,
And sad—for me each day will seem like night.

I'll have no eyes for golden evening, no eyes for nightfall,
Nor as I near the port of Harfleur see a single sail,
But I shall lay upon your tomb, as soon as I get there,
A holly spray and heather all in flower.

June Nights

The summer day is done, and meadows fling
Narcotic perfumes over everything.
We are alert, though we may close an eye;
Still listening, we sleep transparently.

Now shadows look more soft, and stars more bright.
The sky is tinted with a ghost of light.
And gentle dawn seems restlessly to roam,
Waiting for morning, round the heavens' dome.

From "Contemplations"

Life; conversation; overhead clouds, sky.
Books you enjoy by sages long gone by.
Read Virgil and read Dante; then go out
On an excursion to some charming spot.
Laughter; the inn; adventures on the way;
A woman's passing glance fills you with joy.
You loved, you are loved; greatest of all goods
A king might envy! Birds sing in the woods.
You wake up in the morning to embraces—
Mother's, sister's, daughter's smiling faces.
Eat breakfast, read the paper, thinking of
The usual subjects: hope and work and love.
Life with its passions rises like a cloud;
You toss your words to many a solemn crowd;
Confronting your desires and your fate,
You feel both weak and strong, both small and great,
Helplessly tossed by all the winds that blow;
You mourn, you celebrate; things come and go;
Forward, then backward, constantly you strive . . .
And then the deep vast silence of the grave!

Boaz Asleep

Boaz had lain down to sleep, worn out.
All day with other threshers he had toiled,
Then made a bed in his accustomed spot
And slept beside the bushels he had filled.

Owner of fields of barley and of corn,
This man was rich, yet wanted to do right.
The water in his mill ran free of smut;
Nor did hellfire in his smithy burn.

His beard flowed silver as an April stream.
No greed or hatred flourished in his crop.
When he spied some poor gleaners passing, "Stop,"
He'd order. "Leave a few ears out for them."

Pure, far from paths of crookedness he strode,
Both character and garb with candor glowing.
His sacks of grain were fountains overflowing
For every poor wayfarer on the road.

A master and a kinsman kind yet strong,
Careful but generous with his estate,
Boaz drew women's glances—not the young.
Young men are handsome, but old men are great.

Old men move back toward their origin,
Depart from change, approach eternity;
Young men's eyes gleam with fire, as we see,
But with a softer radiance old eyes shine.

*

So Boaz was asleep among his people.
The millstones looked like ruins of a temple,
The slumbering gleaners looked like sculpture too;
And all this happened very long ago.

Israel was ruled by judges in those days.
Tent-dwelling nomads, people fearfully
Shrank from the giant footprints they could see.
The recent flood had softened earth to ooze.

*

Sleeping such sleep as Jacob must have had,
Or Judith, Boaz drowsed beneath his bower.
The gate of heaven chanced to be ajar;
A dream crept down and lighted on his head.

And in this dream he saw a mighty oak
Sprung from his loins, up to blue heaven growing;
A race of people climbed it link by link
Like a long chain to where a god was dying

(At its roots, a king was singing). He
Wondered in his dream, "How can this be?
My sum of years now far exceeds four-score;
I have no sons, and have a wife no more.

It's many years since she with whom I lay
Has left, O Lord, my couch to sleep with Thee;
And we are still entwined like people wed,
She partly living and I partly dead.

Impossible! A people spring from me?
How could I be the father of a son?
Youth is triumphant with each new-fledged dawn,
Each morning bursts from night like victory,

But old men shake like trees when winds are howling.
Widowed and aged, upon me night is falling,
O God! My soul inclines toward the brink
As thirsty oxen bend their brows to drink."

So spoke Boaz in his sleep to God,
Turning his sleep-drenched eyes toward the sky.
A cedar fails to sense a rose nearby;
He didn't sense a woman near his bed.

*

While he was sleeping, Ruth, a Moabite,
Had lain down at the feet of Boaz, breast
Bared, and hoping for some unknown light
When daybreak should awaken in the east.

Boaz had no idea that she was there,
And Ruth had no presentiment of God's will.
Sweetness drifted from the asphodel;
From Galgala soft breezes floated near.

Nuptial, grand, and solemn was the night.
Angels must have flown discreetly through
The darkness; one could barely snatch a sight
Of something wing-shaped, flickering, and blue.

Boaz's soft breathing made a sound
Mingled with brooks that tumble over moss.
This month Nature showed her sweetest face.
Each hilltop with lilies now was crowned.

Ruth was dreaming, Boaz sleeping. Earth
Was black. The distant tinkling of a bell . . .
Enormous goodness down from heaven fell.
At such an hour lions venture forth

To drink. In Ur and Jerimadeth, calm.
Stars enamelled all the deep, dark sky.
In the west a slender crescent shone,
And Ruth, not moving, opening half an eye,

Peered through her veils, and asked herself what great
God, what gleaner of eternal heat
Had negligently tossed before he left
His sickle into heaven's starry loft.

CHARLES BAUDELAIRE
(1821–1867)

Sonnet in Autumn

Your eyes—it's crystal clear—are asking how
We fell into this amorous obsession.
Sweetheart, don't ask. Since only contemplation
Of classic beauty satisfies me now,

My heart will keep its scorching secret shut,
That mystic message marked in signs of flame.
You beckon me to bed—thanks all the same.
Passion I loathe, and even worse is thought.

Come to me. But Love lounges in his lair,
Shadowed in ambush; bends his fatal bow.
His whole ingenious arsenal I know:

Dementia, dread—I recognize them all.
And I and you are growing thin and pale
As autumn suns. A chill is in the air.

The Fountain of Blood

A fountain's pulsing sobs—like this my blood
Measures its flowing, so it sometimes seems.
I hear a gentle murmur as it streams;
Where the wound lies I've never understood.

Like water meadows, boulevards are flooded.
Cobblestones, crisscrossed by scarlet rills,
Are islands; creatures come and drink their fill.
Nothing in nature now remains unblooded.

I used to hope that wine could bring me ease,
Could lull asleep my deeply gnawing mind.
I was a fool: the senses clear with wine.

I looked to Love to cure my old disease.
Love led me to a thicket of IVs
Where bristling needles thirsted for each vein.

Romantic Sunset

Sunrise is beautiful, that fresh cool time,
Jovial explosion rapping out "Good day!"
Happy is he who can without dismay
Salute the sunset's somberer sublime.

I've been there. Have seen flower, field, and stream
Melt at that giant heart's titanic beat.
To the horizon—quick! before it's late,
Too late to catch a final slanting beam!

But the withdrawing god I chase in vain;
Overwhelming Night begins her reign,
Shady and damp and wafting unknown ills;

A floating scent of charnel-house prevails.
Edging along a black polluted lake,
My squeamish foot squashes a toad? a snake?

Retreat

Come in, sweet Sadness, take your ease, sit back.
You asked for twilight—see! and here it is,
Enveloping the city in its mist,
Soothing to some, to others an attack.

Leave millions squirming under Pleasure's sway.
Flicking his whip, that cruel bully drives
Them to fresh orgies. Oh, what sordid lives!
Come here, dear Sadness, take my hand—away,

Goodbye to all that. Look, the years gone by
Are leaning down from Heaven's balcony.
Out of the sea Regret arises, smiles;

The sun curls up to die. For miles and miles
A shroud unfurls along the eastern sky.
Listen, my darling, Night is walking by.

A Taste for Nothingness

Drab soul, enamored once of battle's flame,
Hope used to spur you on; Hope has turned cool.
Nothing is left. Lie down—no need for shame,
Old nag that stumbles at each obstacle.

Give in, my heart, and sleep your brutish fill.

Battered spirit, aged pirate, left
Lukewarm alike by love and argument,
No clashing steel nor woodwinds' soft lament
Can rouse a heart so utterly bereft.

Even the spring has lost her fragrant breath.

Time blanks me out each instant, as a storm
Covers a rigid corpse with miles of white.
The round world turns below me—distant sight;
I want no mountain hut to keep me warm.

Avalanche, pick me up in your long arm.

Dialogue

You glow with beauty like an autumn sky,
But sadness rinses over me like water.
Even at low tide, a memory
Sticks to my sullen mouth. The taste is bitter.

In vain your hand slides down my ruined chest.
Sweet, what you want has all been pulled apart
By slavering carnivores. A bloody feast
Has hollowed out what used to be my heart.

My heart—a palace mobbed by drunken scum,
Mad marauders shrieking through each room.

Around your throat is swimming what perfume . . .

Your fiery eyes look murderously bright,
Beauty, so satisfy your appetite:
Whatever scraps you find still whole, consume.

Misty Sky

Your gaze is like a wall of mist, its hue
Mysteriously changing (gray? green? blue?);
Now dreamy-soft, now hard as steel, your eye
Reflects the lazy pallor of the sky.

Yours is the heat of thick white hours, ripe
For the overloaded heart to break,
When nerves tormented by a nameless ache
Hurl insults at a mind still sound asleep.

You resemble a horizon lit
By suns of misty seasons. Sopping wet
Resplendent landscape! Shafts of light unfold
From the gray sky and turn you into gold.

Love, weather—each a perilous enchanter—
To which distinctive freeze will I succumb?
Or can I coax from adamantine winter
Pleasures as sharp as ice and steel are numb?

The Offended Moon

Ancestrally adored, O Moon, above
Those far blue landscapes where a starry train
Follows your footsteps and attends your throne,
Cynthia, light to many a cozy cave,

Do you see the couples bedded down?
Through gaping mouths their teeth gleam wet and white.
Do you see poets wrestling to write
And, in the meadows, amorous vipers twine?

Robed in yellow, silent, once again
Will you spend nights from sunset until dawn
Kissing poor withered old Endymion?

Lateborn child, I see your mother lean
Before the mirror, painting that same breast
You as an infant suckled and caressed!

The Self-Tormentor

Dispassionate—no rage or hate—
Clean as a slaughterer's my stroke
Will slam you, Moses at the rock!
And from your eyes—oh, they'll be wet—

Anguish will gush in such a stream
It could make any desert bloom.
Fancy-fed, my hopes and fears
Will splash in pools of your salt tears.

As a boat ventures out too far,
My drunken heart will echo back
Your precious sobs, their throbbing like
A drum tattoo announcing war!

For I'm—I know it—a false note
In the music of the spheres,
Thanks to the irony that leers
And clings forever at my throat.

She shrieks, and it's my stolen voice!
What's her black venom but my gore?
I am the monstrous mirror where
The hideous hag beholds her face!

I'm cut flesh and knife-wielding hand!
I am the slap! I am the cheek!
I am the broken limbs, the rack,
And executioner and condemned!

Nourished on nothing but my gore,
Of that forsaken crew am I,
Condemned to laugh eternally—
But as for smiling—*nevermore*.

Song in Autumn

I

It's almost time to plunge into the chill
Season of shadows. Summer warmth, farewell!
I hear funereal thumpings; winter's wood
Is being dumped—already!—in the yard.

Ruthless winter will reclaim my soul
With spite, frustration, drudgery, and dread
That like the sun locked in its arctic hell
My heart will freeze—a chunk of icy red.

I hear, and shudder at it, logs crash down;
No scaffolding in progress could sound more
Foreboding. My imagination's worn
As by a battering-ram's relentless war.

Lulled by these monotonous blows, I'd swear
Workmen were hammering shut a coffin. Where?
And whose? Now summer's given way to fall,
This ghostly sound keeps echoing Farewell.

II

Although I love your long green eyes, my dear,
Everything tastes bitter now to me.
Love and lovemaking—nothing can compare
With memories of sunlight on the sea.

Yet please do love me anyway. I still—
Scapegrace and ingrate—crave your tendernesses
Mother-lover-sisterlike, caresses
Precious as sunset, and ephemeral.

For none of this will last. My grave is here.
Let me, head resting in your lap, drink in
The golden glow of autumn, and bemoan
Bygone summer's shimmering white air.

The Jewels

My clever mistress in her naked grace
Kept on her jewels, whose rich accompaniment
Lent her the air, bedizened and content,
Of Moorish slaves at a triumphant feast.

Precious stones' and metals' coruscation
Utterly seduces me; I swoon,
Ecstatic as at my own honeymoon,
When sound and light make nuptial celebration.

So lazily she lay and smiled at me.
Her sofa was a cliff, and I, the sea,
Subtle and deep, was swept toward her side
Higher and higher by an amorous tide.

A tigress tamed, she'd fix her eyes on me
And then abstractedly would change position;
Ingenuousness and lubricity
Added charm to each fresh transformation,

For arms and legs and thighs and flanks—all these,
Glossily gleaming, undulous as a swan,
Floated before my fascinated gaze.
Her belly and her breasts, grapes of my vine,

Softly as angels troubled my repose,
But angels whose intent was to destroy
That solitary haven, my soul's joy,
By infiltrating every private place.

I thought I saw a new creation: chest
A beardless boy's, a woman's hips below—
Lavish foundation for that slender waist—
And all the rouged and swarthy skin aglow!

The lamp was going out, and knew it. Embers,
Sighing, breaking, flaming in their fall,
Provided our sole light. Each glowing coal
Flooded with blood her skin's translucent amber!

Voyage to Cythera

Free as a bird and joyfully my heart
Soared up among the rigging, in and out;
Under a cloudless sky the ship rolled on
Like an angel drunk with brilliant sun.

"That dark, grim island there—which would that be?"
"Cythera," we're told, "the legendary isle
Old bachelors tell stories of and smile.
There's really not much to it, you can see."

O place of many a mystic sacrament!
Archaic Aphrodite's splendid shade
Lingers above your waters like a scent
Infusing spirits with an amorous mood.

Worshipped from of old by every nation,
Myrtle-green isle, where each new bud discloses
Sighs of souls in loving adoration
Breathing like incense from a bank of roses

Or like a dove *roo-coo*ing endlessly . . .
No; Cythera was a poor infertile rock,
A stony desert harrowed by the shriek
Of gulls. And yet there was something to see:

This was no temple deep in flowers and trees
With a young priestess moving to and fro,
Her body heated by a secret glow,
Her robe half-opening to every breeze;

But coasting nearer, close enough to land
To scatter flocks of birds as we passed by,
We saw a tall cypress-shaped thing at hand—
A triple gibbet black against the sky.

Ferocious birds, each perched on its own meal,
Were madly tearing at the thing that hung
And ripened; each, its filthy beak a drill,
Made little bleeding holes to root among.

The eyes were hollowed. Heavy guts cascading
Flowed like water halfway down the thighs;
The torturers, though gorged on these vile joys,
Had also put their beaks to use castrating

The corpse. A pack of dogs beneath its feet,
Their muzzles lifted, whirled and snapped and gnawed;
One bigger beast amidst this jealous lot
Looked like an executioner with his guard.

O Cytherean, child of this fair clime,
Silently you suffered these attacks,
Paying the penalty for whatever acts
Of infamy had kept you from a tomb.

Grotesquely dangling, somehow you brought on—
Violent as vomit rising from the chest,
Strong as a river bilious to taste—
A flow of sufferings I'd thought long gone.

Confronted with such dear remembered freight,
Poor devil, now it was my turn to feel
A panther's slavering jaws, a beak's cruel drill—
Once it was my flesh they loved to eat.

The sky was lovely, and the sea divine,
But something thick and binding like a shroud
Wrapped my heart in layers of black and blood:
Henceforth this allegory would be mine.

O Venus! On your isle what did I see
But my own image on the gallows tree?
O God, give me the strength to contemplate
My own heart, my own body without hate!

The Swan

I

Andromache, I think of you! This poor
Rivulet where your fabled sorrows gleam,
This downscale Simois where as of yore
Your widow's tears forever swell the stream

Has watered my green memory as well,
Suddenly, at the Place du Carrousel.
Mercurial as human feelings are,
The shapes of cities alter faster far:

Old Paris is no more. I only see
Huts full of bric-a-brac in my mind's eye,
Barrels heaped up, and columns whose rough stone
Splashes of muddy water have turned green.

Caged animals were on display just there;
And there I saw once in the clear cold dawn
When early workers raise a hurricane
Of blackish dust in the still silent air,

A swan. Out of its cage, it dragged its feet
Along the bone-dry sidewalk; glossy white
Pinions trailed the pebbles in its wake.
Near a dry brook-bed opening its beak,

Skittishly flirting feathers in a bath
Of dust, and heartsick for its native lake,
"O water, rain on me! O thunder, break!"
The wretched swan was saying. Fatal myth

Emblazoned like an emblem in the sky—
The tremulous writhing neck, the avid head
Outstretched to tell its troubles straight to God—
Cruel and ironic, still in my mind's eye!

II

Paris changes, not my old distress.
New buildings in construction, scaffoldings,
My memories with their stony heaviness,
Old districts—all are now symbolic things.

Thus before the Louvre even now
The image rises: my great swan, its motions
Dignified, mad as any displaced person's,
Obsessed with endless longing—then of you,

Andromache! No longer sheltered in
Your lost lord's arms, slave of Achilles' son,
You huddle in an ecstasy of grief
To mourn for Hector—Helenus's wife!

I think of a consumptive Negress, gaunt
And haggard, scouring the filthy street
For the lost palm trees of her tropic haunt,
For Africa behind a wall of sleet.

Of losses that can never be made good,
Never! of people draining a whole gulf
Of grief, yes, suckling Sorrow like a wolf;
Of skinny orphans who like flowers fade!

So in the forest of my mind's exile
An ancient memory blows its horn. The sound
Conjures up sailors shipwrecked on an isle,
And prisoners, victims, others without end!

To a Passing Lady

In the street's uproar I stood deaf and dumb.
Dressed in deepest black, a lady passed,
Stately, grief-stricken, fingertip and thumb
Lifting up the black swag of her dress.

What dignity—a statue's grace of limb!
I stood there like an idiot, drinking in
Her pallid glance, the sky before a squall—
Such sweetnesses enslave, and pleasures kill!

As lightning rends the darkness, such was your
Look, so piercing I was born again.
Must our reunion be in heaven, then—

Out there, too far, too late, or nevermore?
The other's destination neither of us knew.
But ah, you recognized my love for you!

The Sun

When the cruel sun more and more fiercely beats
Meadows and rooftops, fields and city streets
Where behind each building's shuttered face
Who knows what orgies may be taking place,
I and my fencing foil take exercise,
Hunting out rhymes where each one, hidden, lies.
Stumbling over—are these words or stones?—
I may come face to face with my own lines.

This foster-father, pallor's enemy,
Sets poems swelling like the buds of May,
Melts sorrows and dissolves them into air,
And fills my thoughts with honey everywhere.
He whose force transforms the hobbling cripple
Into a creature radiant and supple
Is he at whose command the harvests yield
Their bounty in the heart's immortal field.

When, poetlike, he ventures to the street,
He gives each vilest thing a better fate,
Unostentatious king who makes his state
Visit to both the wretched and the great.

The Promises of a Face

From the arched brows in your pale face, my dear,
Shadows seem to fall;
The thoughts your eyes, however black, inspire
Are hardly dark at all.

Reflecting darkness from that springy mane
Of jet-black hair, your eyes
Speak to me in a caressing tone:
"Lover of shapeliness,

If you desire to pursue the path
Of hope and hunger we have opened up,
Here is how to test its fleshly truth
Below the navel, at the buttocks' slope.

Above, of course, are generous globes of breast
With bronze medallions nippled,
And then beneath the belly, like a nest
Velvety, swarthy, stippled,

A lavish fleece, the nether sister to
Your wealth of flowing hair,
Wiry and supple and as thick as you,
Black night without a star!"

The Voice

My cradle stood against the bookcase, Babel
Of murky voices. Novel, science, fable,
Greek dust, and Latin ashes made one stew.
When I was tall as a big folio,
Two voices spoke to me. The first was firm,
Also seductive: "This world's full of charm.
What I can do for you, my boy, is make
Your hunger equal to this endless cake."
The other: "Come to dreamland! Come explore
Beyond the merely possible and known!"
This voice was like a wind along the shore,
A rootless phantom singing on its own
With a caressing, terrifying sound.
I answered "Yes! Sweet voice!" And so began
Whatever you might call it—say my wound
And my fatality. Behind the scenes
Of this enormous stage, in an abyss
Of blackness, I see other worlds than this.
Privileged victim of a clear-eyed fate,
I drag along with serpents at my feet.
And since that time the prophet within me
Loves above all the desert and the sea;
I laugh at funerals and weep at feasts,
And in the sourest wine find some sweet taste;
Many a humdrum fact I call a lie,
And fall in holes through gazing at the sky.
My Voice consoles me: "Keep your mad dreams, far
Fairer than than the dreams of wise men are!"

Invitation to a Journey

Sister, lover, mate,
Imagine the delight
Of going off together, just we two,
To make love lazily,
To love and then to die
In a far country that looks just like you!
Skies veiled in damp
Dim the sun's lamp
With just the same appeal
For me as your eyes
Which, treacherous,
Gleam right through your tears' veil!

Even beauty there is made to measure,
Beauty and luxury and calm and pleasure.

Glossy as from
The hand of Time,
The furniture of our room;
And flowers rare
That fill the air
With amber-scented bloom,
And ceilings that gaze
In a mirror's glaze,
And the walls with splendors hung,
In secret all

Would speak to the soul
In her beautiful native tongue.

Even beauty there is made to measure,
Beauty and luxury and calm and pleasure.

On the canals
With lowered sails
Lie ships that love to roam;
But your desire
Has brought them here
From scattered harbors home.
The setting sun
Folds harbor, town,
And all the scene in deep
Purple and gold
And soon the world
In warm light falls asleep.

Even beauty there is made to measure,
Beauty and luxury and calm and pleasure.

The Vampire's Metamorphoses

Squirming like a serpent in a fire
And kneading up her breasts a little higher,
The woman now let words like honey drip
Out of the ripe red berries of her lips:
"My mouth is luscious. Deep within a bed
I know how consciences can be mislaid.
On my triumphant bosom old men dry
Their tears—I make each giggle like a boy.
For those who chance to see me naked, I
Become sun, moon, and stars—yes, the whole sky!
Sir, so ingenious am I in my charms
That when I take a man in my strong arms
And let him nip and bite and kiss a breast
Modest and brazen, and robust and frail,
Even the pillows seem to sigh with lust.
For my sake angels would go straight to hell."

When she had sucked my very marrow dry,
And I was turning toward her languidly
To kiss her in return, I—what was this?
A sticky leather bottle full of pus.
Shocked, I shut my eyes in frigid fear
And opened them again to see, quite clear,
Where next to me a figurine had stood,
Sturdy and strong from lavish draughts of blood,
Were now chaotic gibberings of bone.
Skeletal chips creaked like a weathervane,
Or like, high on an iron pole, some sign
Flapping all night while winds of winter whine.

The Hair

Fleece falling to her neck like so much foam,
Curls drenched with nonchalance as with perfume!
To charm to life tonight the murky room
Of memories nestled in this head of hair,
I want to shake it like a scarf in the air!

Drowsy Asia, Africa's bright heat,
A whole world distant, absent, all but dead
Lives in your murky depths, enchanted shade!
Music sets many other souls in motion;
Mine bathes itself in your sweet-scented ocean.

Strong tresses, be the wave that carries me
Down to where lusty trees yield languidly
As men to the long ardors of each day!
A dazzling dream drifts through your ebony
Current: sails, rowers, masts against the sky,

No less than a whole harbor where my soul
Of scent and sound and sight can drink its fill
And in whose gold and satin waters lie
Great vessels that with open arms enjoy
The endless heat that trembles in the sky.

My love-intoxicated head I'll smother
In this black ocean where there hides the Other
Whose swarthy swell will rock me like a mother;
I'll find my way to you again, rich leisure,
Endlessly lulled by laziness and pleasure!

Cloud-blue hair, a thousand shadows' home,
You give me back the azure of the dome,
The sky itself! And with each strand of hair
I breathe, my senses stagger more and more
At mingled musk and coconut and tar.

I'll sow a ton of jewels in your hair—
Rubies, sapphires, pearls—so my desire
Will find in you fulfillment evermore,
Oasis of my dreams, O drinking gourd
Brimful of wine where memories are stored.

Blessing

When by Omnipotence's dread decree
The Poet is born into this yawning scene,
His mother, frightened into blasphemy,
Shakes a pathetic fist at the unseen:

"Ugh! Better to have spawned a vipers' nest
Than have this vile absurdity to nurse!
Damn the night whose temporary lust
Made me conceive this object of remorse!

But since among all women I've been blessed—
My husband looks at me with deep disgust—
And can't consign this runty misfit to
The fire like a guilty billet-doux,

I'll make the cursed cause of my distress
Suffer my anger at Your wickedness;
So thoroughgoing will my tortures be,
Not one sick bud shall grace this wretched tree!"

Thus, swallowing the spume of her own hate,
Not understanding the designs of Fate,
She readies deep in Hell ahead of time
The stake used only for maternal crime.

And yet invisibly an angel broods
Over the child; sun succors the outcast,
And in his very water and his food
Nectar and ambrosia leave a taste.

He chats with clouds, his playmate is the breeze,
Troubles he turns to charming melodies;
His tutelary spirit weeps to see
Him happy as a songbird in a tree.

People he'd like to love watch him with fear,
Or, taking courage from his calm, they try
To rival one another's cruelty:
Can no one wring from him a single tear?

Into his bread and wine these hypocrites
Smuggle ashes and great gobs of spit;
Whatever he has touched they feign to shun,
Even the path his feet have trod upon.

His wife goes shrilling through the public squares:
"Since it is my beauty he adores,
I'll imitate the pagan gods of old
And have myself like them encased in gold;

And then—oh, the incense, the genuflections!
Wines and sweetmeats! Glutted with worship, mad,
I'll see if I can filch what he owes God—
His simple-minded duties and affections!

When godless farces start to pall, I plan
To touch him with my feeble little hand;
My nails, like harpies' claws, can pull apart
The flesh and find a way straight to his heart.

Trembling like a fledgling in its nest,
This heart I'll rip all bloody from his breast,
And for a tidbit to some faithful hound
Disdainfully I'll toss it on the ground."

The Poet sees a glorious throne on high
And lifts his arms, ecstatic, to the sky;
The brilliant vistas he's at home among
Keep him from noticing the angry throng.

"Blessed be God who doles out agony
For all our sins—a heavenly dispensation,
And one whose best and purest distillation
Prepares the strong for heavenly joys to be!

Among the ranks of sainted populations,
I know the Poet has a special place,
And that You will invite me face to face
To feast with Virtues, Thrones, and Dominations!

Pain is the sole nobility I know
Which earth and hell can never overflow;
All time, and the whole cosmos, I must braid
Into a mystic crown for my own head.

But the lost jewels of antiquity,
Pearls rich and strange, and metals from the sea,
Could never hold the dimmest candle to
My dazzling diadem, even if set by You.

For my crown will be formed of purest light
Forged from those primal beams whose source is holy,
And of which mortal eyes, however bright,
Are only mirrors, murky, melancholy!"

Beauty

My beauty is a reverie in stone.
My breast, where each is shattered in his turn,
Inspires the poet with a love as mute
And everlasting as an element.

Mysterious sphinx whose kingdom is the sky,
My frozen heart is wrapped in pure swan-down.
I hate all gestures that disturb my calm,
And never do I laugh and never cry.

Faced with the splendid attitudes I seem
To have taken over from antiquity,
Poets will keep on poring over me,

Such meek admirers. For I offer them
A limpid mirror, one that purifies:
The endless clarity of my wide eyes.

Lethe

Unfeeling, cruel lover, come,
Sweet tiger, beast with sullen air.
My trembling fingers long to comb
Through that thick heavy stuff, your hair.

Your perfume lingers in your skirt.
Burying my head there, I'll inhale—
Sweet as a fading flower is sweet—
The odor of a love gone stale.

Rather than living, let me sleep!
Delicious, in that deathlike dream,
To let my kisses smother up
Your lovely body's coppery gleam.

And nothing can so quickly quell
My sobbing as your bed's black hole;
Your lips are twin oblivions,
And through your kisses Lethe runs.

Old pleasures usher illness in.
Martyrdom diagnosed, I yield,
A hapless victim, meek and mild,
Whose patience goads my virus on.

Opiates for lulling my distress
I take in through the catheter
Like a third nipple in my chest.
Only a heart is lacking there.

Don Juan in Hell

Down in Hell, Don Juan paid Charon's fare
Where the subterranean waters flow;
A brooding beggar with a fearful stare,
Seizing the oars like fate, began to row.

Robes half open, pendulous breasts showing,
Women were writhing under blackish skies;
And like a line of beasts for sacrifice
Behind him trailed a drawn-out sound of lowing.

"My wages!" Sganarelle sniggered. "Where?"
And Don Luis, hand trembling, pointed out
To all the spirits wandering about
The son who poked cruel fun at his white hair.

Black-clad and trembling, chaste and gaunt, meanwhile,
Elvira from her faithless husband seemed
(And lover) to be claiming one last smile
Wherein—long dead—sweet protestations gleamed.

Rigid in armor, a tall man of stone
Stood at the rail, dividing the black flood;
But the calm hero, leaning on his sword,
Gazed at the wake as if he were alone.

Blind Men

Regarding them, recoil in dread, my soul!
Weird as somnambulists, and terrible,
Yet laughable like mannequins, they stare,
Their cloudy glances darting God knows where.

Their eyes, from which the spark divine's been snuffed,
Turn heavenward, as if to gaze far off;
One never sees them stumble, looking down,
Heads bent as if to study every stone.

And thus they cross invisibility,
That brother to eternal silence. See,
O City, who around us laugh, sing, scream,

Victim of pleasure dragged to each extreme,
I too go groping; but—more dazed than they—
I ask what blind men look for in the sky.

Posthumous Remorse

My shadowy beauty, when they lay you deep
In a black marble monument to sleep
And when your only boudoir is a cave
Dripping with rain, your country house the grave;

When the same stone that weighs down thighs and chest
Formerly lovely in their nonchalance
Will freeze your heart's desires in your breast
And halt those feet that stepped so nimbly once,

Recipient of my endless dreams, that tomb
During the long nights sleep is banished from
(Poet and grave—they go together well)

Will ask you why you never took it in,
Light-headed wench, just why dead people wail.
And like remorse a worm will gnaw your skin.

"Her Garments' Iridescent Undulation . . ."

Her garments' iridescent undulation
Turns each separate step into a dance,
Like snakes which conjurors in a sacred trance
Charm onto sticks with rhythmic agitation.

Like deserts—their bleak sand and blue terrain
Indifferent alike to mortal pain—
Or like the hollows in the ocean's gulf,
With that much human warmth she preens herself.

Highly polished minerals make her eyes.
And in her strange symbolic nature lies
(Where sphinx and radiant angel alternate

And everything is gold, steel, diamonds, light)
The frigid star of her sterility
Shining forever useless in the sky.

The Owls

Under their cover of black yews
Brooding like gods from far away
The owls have perched themselves in rows
With a flash from each red eye

And motionless will stay right there
Until the melancholy hour
When, pushing off the sun's last slant,
Shadows will settle on the land.

Let's learn from their behavior
That in this world we ought to fear
Aimlessly darting here and there;

The man enthralled by passing faces
Is punished each and every day
For having wanted to change places.

Carrion

Do you remember, dear, what you and I
  Saw? It was a lovely summer day.
Just off the path a carcass, thing of dread,
  Perched on a pebbly bed.

Legs in the air like a lubricious wench,
  Oozing out poison, baking in the sun,
Splayed with an air of pleasure overdone
  Its belly brewing many a vile stench.

As if instructed "Roast until well done,"
  The sunlight trembled on this rottenness,
Paying Nature back with interest
  For her magnificent construction.

Upon this carrion blossoming like a flower
  The sky looked blandly down.
You thought that you might swoon,
  Such was its putrescence's sheer power.

Around the belly, swarms of flies were humming.
  Squadrons of maggots kept on blackly coming
In battle lines that flowed as thick as soup
  Over and under every wretched scrap.

Like a wave, these creatures rose and fell,
Surged and splashed and bubbled into froth,
As if the carrion, somehow living still,
Multiplied itself with every breath.

Uncanny music from this population
Came forth, a sound like wind or running water,
Or like the grains of wheat a winnower
Shakes out in his fan with rhythmic motion.

The shapes effaced themselves, became no more
Than rough drafts, hesitant,
Half-finished, of a painter who's unsure
Himself of what he meant.

Behind some rocks a bitch full of unease
Was peering at us, poised to leap and seize
And chomp and chew and slaver once again
Any flesh still clinging to the bone.

And yet you too will come to this decay.
Decomposition waits for you one day,
Star of my eyes, my nature's sovereign sun,
Beloved angel, O my passion.

Yes, queen of all the graces! You also,
    When every ceremony is complete,
Under the flowering grasses you will go,
    Down with the bones to rot.

Go and tell the scavengers from me,
    As their voracious kisses eat you up,
That I have managed to retain the shape
    And beauty of my loves as they decay.

The Seven Old Men

Here specters pluck at passers-by. O teeming
City, huge, mysteriously dreaming
Even in daylight! Strange sap secretly
Flows through each constricted passageway.

One morning I was down in the dark street
Whose houses—the mist lent them extra height—
Looked tall as twin banks of a swollen stream.
As actors' moods can infiltrate a scene,

Vile yellow fog crept all along the ground.
I strained for fortitude, the hero's part,
Striving to banish weakness from my heart,
Trudging the track where lumbering tumbrils groaned.

Abruptly an old man appeared to me
In rags the color of the sodden sky.
Plenty of charity would have come his way
But for the wicked glimmer in his eye,

Jaundiced and evil as if steeped in gall.
At his glance the temperature fell.
His matted beard, as rigid as a sword,
Jutted out as that of Judas would.

His legs were at right angles to his back;
He wasn't bent, but broken altogether.
A final touch was added by his stick
So that he hobbled like a crippled creature

Or Jew on three legs. Through the muddy slush
He waded heavily as if to crush
A layer of dead bodies underfoot
Not out of carelessness but out of hate.

Another one was coming—beard, stick, all—
Specter in each detail identical!
A senile twin had spring from the same hell.
They marched in tandem toward some secret goal.

Innocent victim of an evil scheme
Or dreadful chance, abashed and horrified,
One by one I counted seven of him!
The sinister old man had multiplied.

Whoever laughs at my anxiety
And doesn't shudder out of sympathy,
Please understand: for all their frailty,
These monsters would live on eternally,

Or so it seemed. Could I have borne to see
An eighth advancing inexorably,
Filthy Phoenix, at once sire and brood?
I turned my back on the whole damned parade.

As fitful drunks with double vision stagger,
I hurried home and locked the door in horror,
Exhausted, sick, confusion in my brain,
Mystery, absurdity my twofold pain.

Vainly my reason tried to take command
Over the tempest howling through my mind.
Abandoned, rudderless, my soul danced free
Over a desolate and shoreless sea.

The Voyage

I

The child in love with maps and prints desires
Nothing less than the whole universe.
How huge the world by lamplight! Equally,
How tiny in the eyes of memory!

One fine day we leave, our brains on fire,
Our hearts puffed up with rancor and desire,
And following the ocean's rhythms, we
On finite seas lull our infinity,

Some pleased to leave their fearful native place;
Others, the nightmares of their childhood days;
Some drown, astrologers, in a woman's eyes,
Perfumed, perfidious, poison sorceress.

In order not to be transformed to beasts,
They gulp down space and light and skies that burst
With heat. And ice that gnaws them, suns that roast
Slowly erase the marks where they were kissed.

But true travelers alone depart
In order to be going. Light of heart,
They never try to shrink from destiny.
Not knowing why, "Let's go!" they blithely say.

Cloudlike—for their desires lack boundaries—
As conscripts brood on cannonfire, they dream
Of unknown pleasures, strange immensities
Which the human mind can never name.

II

O God—even in our sleep we roll, we spin
Like balls and tops. Our curiosity
Keeps us in turmoil with the cruelty
Of an angel whipping up the sun.

Strange destiny—our goal keeps moving on.
It's nowhere, so it could be anywhere;
And since our hopefulness is ever green,
We race toward rest—madmen as we all are!

Scouring the seas for what enthralled us, we
Hear a voice hallooing from the deck:
"Land ahoy!" then the mad lookout's cry:
"Love . . . glory . . . happiness!" Shit—it's a rock!

Every island that the lookout cries
Is an Eldorado Fate holds out;
Imagination's dazzled reveries
See only reefs in the clear morning light.

In love with Never-Never Land, poor fool!
Put him in irons or hurl him in the sea,
Besotted tar whose dream America
Only makes reality seem cruel.

The aged vagabond who shuffles by
Broods of enchantments with his head held high,
Glimpsing another Capua each time
His candle flickers in the filthy slime.

III

Amazing travelers, in whose limpid look
We read your history like an open book,
Show us where your memory's caskets are,
And your stored jewels, compounds of stars and air!

No sails, no steam—let's just be on our way!
And please relieve our prison cells' ennui:
On our taut minds let your bright memories play,
Framed only by the boundaries of day.

What did you see?

IV

We saw the stars. And then
Sand. Plenty of water—waves and foam.
Despite disasters no one had foreseen,
Things were as dull as if we'd stayed at home.

Glory of sun upon a violet sea,
Glory of cities sunset flushes red
Lit in our hearts a corresponding need
To plunge into the sky's serenity.

Rich citadels and farflung countrysides
Faded before the mystical appeal
Of what chance fashions out of passing clouds.
And our desire made us want more still!

Actual enjoyment renders each wish strong.
Pleasure feeds desire. O lusty tree,
Your tough old bark grows thicker day by day,
Your growing branches stretch toward the sun!

Will you shoot up forever, splendid tree,
High as a cypress? Anyhow, with care
We've plucked some souvenirs you can admire,
You who adore all things from far away!

Before what trumpery idols we've bowed down,
Their thrones with galaxies of gems ablaze.
The fairy splendor of their palaces
Would bankrupt anyone to dream upon!

Costumes before which the poor mind reels,
Women who paint their teeth as well as nails,
Like acrobats by their own snakes beguiled—

V

And then, what next?

VI

You talk just like a child!

One thing everywhere we stumbled on
Whether or not we sought it. Up and down
The fatal ladder's every blessed rung
Were dreary visions of eternal sin.

Women, degraded, stupid, vain, and lewd,
Self-worshippers with no hint of irony;
Men, fragile, harsh, tyrannical, and crude,
Drops in the flood of human misery;

The hangman beaming while the martyr weeps;
Ceremonies savoring of gore;
Poisonous power that through the despot seeps,
Crazed populations begging "Whip us more!"

Several religions more or less like this,
All petitioning Heaven. Holiness
(As a debauchee on down pillows rolls)
Seeks out her pleasure in a bed of nails.

Meanwhile that chatterbox humanity,
Crazy as ever, drunk with vanity,
Shrieks in the desperation of its pain
"O God, I look like you! I curse your name!"

Less feeble are those hardy souls who flee
The herd of prisoners trapped by destiny
And lose themselves in opium's endless snooze . . .
Worldwide and forever, that's the news!

VII

Bitter proves the wisdom we distill
From travel. The world, tedious and small
Now and forever, presents for us to see
Ghastly oases in a vast ennui.

Go or stay? Oh if you can, stay here;
Leave if you must. Hiding or running, we
Fail either way to cheat the enemy,
Time, that dark runner, vigilant and dour.

Like the apostles, like the wandering Jew,
No boat or train is swift enough for them
Fleeing his net. Yet others know somehow
While in their cradles how to slaughter Time.

When finally Time's foot is on our neck,
Our only hope's in shouting "Off we go!"
As once upon a time we sailed away,
Eyes on the horizon, hair blown back.

So we embark upon the shadowy sea,
Our hearts as light as if we were a boy
On his maiden voyage. Voices clear
Yet deathly beckon us: "Come over here,

O would-be lotus eaters! We've rich store
Of delicacies that you hunger for;
Come and get drunk upon the strange delight
Of afternoon that never turns to night."

We recognize the voice—we guess the ghost!
Friends like Pylades open wide their arms.
"Swim toward your Electra, dearest, come!"
Says the one whose knees we once embraced.

VIII

O Death, old captain, it is time. Let's go.
This country is used up. Put out to sea!
Inky black though sky and ocean be,
Our hearts are full of radiance, as you know.

So let your soothing poisons on us flow!
Since such a fire is burning in our skull,
We wish to plumb the depths of Heaven or Hell—
All that's unknown—in search of something *new*!

STÉPHANE MALLARMÉ
(1842–1898)

Anguish

Embodiment of many an old transgression,
Poor fool, I am not here to take possession;
Under the dreariness my kiss leaves there,
I'll tangle no sad tempest in your hair.

I beg your bed to let you slumber deep—
No guilty dreams may roam the sheets, not one!
Tired of lying, enjoy this heavy sleep,
Death's rival expert in oblivion.

Vice, undermining my nobility,
Has branded me, like you, with its sterility.
But a heart lives inside your breast of stone

Unbitten by the tooth of any crime;
While I keep fleeing, haunted by my tomb,
Afraid of dying if I sleep alone.

Summer Sadness

On the beach, O sleeping wrestler,
Sun warms a drowsy bath in your gold hair.
Your alien cheek is where his incense flares;
Into a lovers' potion he stirs tears.

In this white heat, a spell of lazy calm
Saddens my timid kisses. "Will we never,"
You ask, "be mummified as one forever
In some far desert underneath a palm?"

Your hair is flowing like a lukewarm stream
To drown that hovering soul without a qualm
And find your goal of unknown Nothingness!

As for mascara running down your face,
I'll taste it: can it soothe an injured breast
With something like the blue sky's stoniness?

Apparition

In mournful moonlight, seraphim in tears
Held bows amidst a cloudy mass of flowers
And dreamily from sad violas drew
White sobs sliding down the petals' blue.
Your first kiss! This was that precious day.
I was a martyr in my reverie,
Intoxicated by that sad perfume
Which even without drunkenness or gloom
Clings to the heart that's gone in quest of dreams.
I wandered then, eyes on the paving stones,
When on the street of evening, laughingly,
Hair full of sunlight, you appeared to me
As if that fairy in a flittering crown
Of whom as a spoiled child I used to dream
Were through her half-clasped fingers snowing down
Like white bouquets, stars—stars full of perfume!

Windows

Tired of the hospital, whose sad stale smell
Creeps up through the curtains' prissy white
Toward the great crucifix on its blank wall,
The man who's dying pulls himself upright

And haltingly—but not so much to warm
His rottenness as see sun shine on stone—
Drags himself, a pallid skeleton,
Toward the window and its one bright beam.

His mouth, lips fever-cracked, thirsting in vain
For azure (once it breathed its treasure in—
But that was years ago—a sleek young skin),
With one long sour kiss fouls the window pane.

Forgetting holy oils, herbal infusions,
Clock, cough, bed of pain, he gazes out;
When evening dyes the roofs like a contusion,
His eye at the horizon gorged with light

Sees golden galleys beautiful as swans
Asleep on a sweet-smelling purple bay,
Rocking the brown, rich brightness of their lines
In utter peace shot through with memory!

So I, disgusted by the coarse-souled dunce
Who, prey to his own basest appetite
For creature comfort, seeks out more of it
To give the wife who suckles their young ones,

To every window pane escape, therefore,
Where I can turn my back on life and be
Rinsed with eternal dew; and glassily
Gilded by the cool dawn of Evermore,

I gaze and see an angel! and I die
(Whether the glass is art or mystery)
To be reborn! to wear dreams like a crown
In some lost Heaven where Beauty once could bloom.

But the real world—curse it—masters me;
Even in this safe shelter face to face,
The filthy spewings of stupidity
Against the blue sky make me hold my nose.

Acquainted as I am with bitterness,
Might I somehow smash the sullied glass
And even though my wings lack feathers, fly
Away, not fall through all eternity?

Another Fan of Mlle Mallarmé

Dreamer, that I may dive deep
Into delight without a plan,
By artful pretexts learn to keep
My wing clasped firmly in your hand.

Energy captive in each stroke
Moves the horizon gently back
And there blows over you as well
A breath of evening, fresh and cool.

Dizziness! for all of space
Shudders like an enormous kiss
Destined for no one, fit to burst,
Condemned to an eternal thirst.

Paradisiacal, this heat:
From the corner of your mouth
Buried laughter's leaking out
To settle in the deepest pleat.

Sceptre of a rose-red world
Drowsy with evenings of gold,
This winged white object that you hold
Against a flaming bracelet furled.

ARTHUR RIMBAUD
(1854–1891)

MEMORY

I

Clear water; as with childhood's tears of brine,
whiteness of women's bodies; pounce of sun;
a silken mass, pure lilies, banners spread
beneath ramparts defended by some Maid;

angels romp—No . . . a sluggish golden flow,
grass arms, heavy, black, and cool, that sway.
A lady whose blue canopy is sky
commandeers shadows as her drapery.

II

Ah, bubbles, clear on the moist window pane!
With deep pale gold, water is making up
expectant beds. From willows (faded green
children's frocks) birds impudently hop.

Pure eyelid, warm, more golden than a coin,
the marigold—your pledge, Fidelity!—
from its dim mirror envies just at noon
the rose Sphere worshipped in the hot gray sky.

III

In the field Madame stands up too straight
next to workmen softly snowing down;
her parasol takes a clustering flower apart;
children are reading on the flower-strewn green

their leatherbound red book. Alas! He's gone,
like angel flocks dispersing on the road,
away toward the mountain. Dark and cold,
she hurries in the same direction.

IV

For strong young arms in the pure grass, regret!
New moons of April in a virgin bed!
Joy: vacant worksites by the riverside
on August evenings nourishing all this rot!

Now let her weep below the wall! Up there
only a breath of poplars stirs the air.
Like a gray cloth, dull water stretches out;
an old man's barely moving in his boat.

V

Eye of wistful wet whose toy I am,
oh boat I cannot reach, oh too short arm!
Neither that flower there—yellow—nor the other,
that blue one, friendly to the ash-gray water.

Ah, willow pollen that a wing has shaken!
On the reeds, the blossoms long since eaten!
Its chain fast on the bottom, deep in muck,
in this pond my boat forever stuck.

Poets at Seven

Account book shut, the mother walked away
Satisfied and proud. She didn't see
On the lumpy forehead of her son
And in his blue eyes how disgust had won.

The effort of obedience made him sweat.
Intelligent, yes; yet some murky trait
Also emerged, rank, hypocritical.
As he went down the moldy-smelling hall,
He'd stick his tongue out, fists jammed at his thighs,
And spots appeared before his screwed-up eyes.
Open the door to evening and see
Him lounging on the balcony, late day
Still drooping from the rooftops. Summertime
Found him holed up in the cool bathroom
Where, dreaming in uninterrupted peace,
He could inhale the odors of the place.

Winters, the little garden by the house
Used moonlight to rinse off its dailiness.
He'd mash his eye right up against the wall,
Avid for visions, kneeling in the soil,
And hear the moldy trellis creak and sway.
The only kids available to play
Were feeble-minded, wall-eyed, sickly; hid
Their skinny fingers, gold and black with mud,

In the fetid pockets of their shirts.
Conversing with an idiot can be sweet!
When mother noticed these vile friendships, she
Found them appalling; such deep sympathy
Coming from *her* son filled her with surprise.
He mollified her with his false blue gaze.

At seven he wrote novels about life
(Liberty shining in the desert; strife;
Suns; forests; banks; savannahs) with the aid
Of illustrated papers which he read
And blushed at many a laughing southern beauty.
When—eight years old, in cotton frock—a cutie,
The brown-eyed child of workers from next door,
Arrived to wrestle (little warrior!),
They'd tussle in a corner, she would leap
Up on his back and shake her braids; he'd nip
Her buttocks (for she wore no pants or slip);
With fists and nails she'd pummel him, and then
Back in his room he'd smell her skin again.

December Sundays were a source of dread.
At a low table, hair stiff with pomade,
A pale green Bible he was forced to read,
And dreams oppressed him every night in bed.
It wasn't God he loved, but, in the brown
Twilight, smocked workmen coming back to town,
Where a street vendor rapping on a drum
Made the crowd that gathered laugh or groan.
Also erotic meadows were his dream:

Luminous billows, golden youths, perfume
Made tranquil gestures and grew still again.

Dark things above all he delighted in,
So in his bare blue room, the curtains drawn,
Atmosphere pungent with humidity,
He could reread his novel endlessly:
Its sopping forests, clouds like yellow clay,
Its fleshly blossoms opening to the sky,
Vertiginous descents, catastrophe!
Downstairs meanwhile the buzz of neighborhood
Constantly undermined his solitude.
Alone on great rough canvas cloths, he lay
Like a boat about to sail away.

Ophelia

I

Along that calm black wave where the stars rest,
Like a great lily white Ophelia floats,
Floats very slowly in her long gown's nest . . .
Listen! from far-off woods, halloos and shouts.

A thousand years and more, Ophelia's glided
Down the black stream, a phantom clad in white,
And to each breeze of evening has confided
For all those years her mad romantic plight.

Kissing her breasts, the wind spreads out her gown,
Those trailing clothes the waters gently lap;
Upon her shoulder shivering willows weep,
Toward her high dreamy forehead reeds bend down.

Around her crumpled waterlilies sigh.
Sometimes she stirs, in trees still slumbering,
Some nest, whence comes a feeble fluttering.
Mysterious, a song falls from the sky.

II

O pale Ophelia, beautiful as snow,
Poor child, a river bore you off to death!
It was the gales from mountain crags that blow
Out the words "wild freedom" under their breath;

It was the wind that whipped at your long hair
And with strange rustlings filled your reverie;
Your heart that heeded Nature's melody
When night sighed and the trees moaned with despair;

It was the manic rattling of the sea
That cracked your childish, vulnerable heart;
A pale but handsome knight, one April day,
Sat down, poor madman, mutely at your feet!

Heaven! Freedom! Love! Poor child, mad fantasies!
You melted in him, snow on a fire thrown;
The splendor of your visions made you dumb;
The Infinite appalled your mild blue eyes!

III

The Poet says that you return at night
In search of flowers you gathered by starlight;
And that he's seen, her draperies spread wide,
Ophelia like a great white lily glide.

JULES LAFORGUE
(1860–1887)

A Flash over the Abyss

High on a tower, stars surrounded me.
Suddenly zapped by lightning, dizzily
shaking like jelly with alarm and awe,
the riddle of the universe I saw,
and felt its stupefying mystery!
Are we alone? Where am I? Where are we
going—this whirling lump that carries me
along with it? And can I simply die
in total ignorance? Time, tell me why
you flow in one direction! Stop! Look! How
can I be happy? Things could end right now!
What can I say? First, night; then there I was.
What is the universe's primal cause?
Priests are only human, and they know
nothing—like everybody. O God, show
yourself, eternal witness! Tell me why
we live! All's silent. Space will never say.
Stars, wait a minute! I don't want to die!
Think of it—a genius like me
reduced to nothing for eternity!

Winter Sunset

Depressing, the sunset this evening.
Wind in the trees wept like a wretched thing.
Dead wood and dried-up rusty leaves went flying.
Through networks formed by branches dead and dying
there clearly shone the light blue, frigid day.
Lonely and sad, the sovereign of the sky
stepped down. O Sun! Last summer at your setting
gloriously, all heaven seemed igniting,
azure on fire! And now what do we see?
A sickly yellow disk without a ray
at the reddish-streaked horizon die
deserted, and in grim consumptive style,
feebly filling in the clouds' thick chill
with white (but livid); green (but bilious);
old gold, lead gray, dim lilac, faded rose.
And now it's over. Rattling of wind.
Jaundiced and wheezing, the year's days are done,
and Earth to sheer sterility has come.
Her sickly children, bald and skinny, brood
forever on the problems of the void,
and stooped and shivering under piles of scarves
in the dim gaslight of the boulevards
study their absinthe mutely, empty-eyed,
but rallying to snicker bitterly
whenever pregnant women saunter by
with outthrust breasts and bellies, dignified
as temple slaves, but beastly in their pride.

O storms that usher in the final age,
approach! Let loose tornadoes! Tempests, rage!
Take this fouled, gasping planet and sweep clean
its leprous cities, its corrupted men!
Let the nameless residue be thrown
into the void, and let it not be known,
among undying stars' fresh innocence,
what an infected brain our Earth was once!

PAUL VALÉRY
(1871–1945)

Aurora

Confusion and gloom,
My versions of repose,
Dissipate as the room
Is touched with dawn's first rose.
Endowed with new control,
I straighten up my soul
And I begin to pray.
Barely emerged from depths
Of sleep, courageous steps
Move toward the light of day.

Hail! I salute you, twin
Similitudes, who each—
Smiling, asleep, akin—
Shine out from common speech
And who contain all these
Sounds like a hive of bees
While tremblingly I hold
Onto the lowest end
And cautiously ascend
A ladder of pure gold.

How dawn's illumination
Awakens drowsy groups,
Enlivening with motion
What slumbered as mere shapes!
Some scintillate, some yawn.

Vague fingers stray along
A comb, mother of pearl,
Just surfacing from dreams,
Whose lazy mistress seems
To link it with this world.

Soulful ideas at play,
I've caught you at it now!
What did you do till day
To fend off your ennui?
They answer: "We're forever
Benign. Our presence never
Has betrayed your house.
Not leaving you alone,
We secret spiders spin
Webs in your dwelling place.

Are you not drunk with joy
To see what we have wrought?
Silk suns unnumbered we
Have woven on your thought.
See how we stretch the weft
Over your gloomy cleft,
And with such simple strands
Catch innocent creation
In our reticulation
Of gently trembling bonds."

Their cobwebs' subtle clinging
I break, and go to find
Oracles for my singing
In the forest of my mind.
The universe decrees
That every soul should seize
The height of its desire,
Heeding the faintest sigh;
Lips parted, even I
Sense shudderings in the air.

My shady vineyards here,
Cradles of every chance—
How many forms appear
Before my dreamy glance!
Each green leaf's offering
Is a refreshing spring.
I drink the soft sound in;
For so much juicy flesh
I have no other wish
Than time to taste again.

I have no fear of thorns!
Waking is hard but good.
These mental whips and scorns
Decree a cautious mood.
No charm can cast its spell
Unless it wounds as well
The charmer who in pain
Acknowledges what scars him.
His blood drawn reassures him
The suffering's his own.

By limpid light caressed,
The pool I now draw near.
Borne up along its breast,
My Hope is bathing there,
Haloed above the mass
Of water, clear as glass.
Its power lets her know
What mystic depths achieve
Union within the wave.
She shudders head to toe.

The Friendly Wood

Side by side along the way
We held hands. Our thoughts were pure.
No need of anything to say.
Even the flowers were obscure.

Like affianced and fiancé,
We walked alone in the green night,
Partaking of that fairy fruit
The moon, a friend to such as we.

Then among roses we lay dead,
Far away and all alone
In the sweet-shadowed murmuring glade;

There under the enormous sky
We found ourselves in tears—O my
Partner in silence, dear companion!

Helen

Ah, azure! From the caves of death I come
To hear the hollow waves break in a line
And see at dawn the galleys reappear
Out of the shadows, oar by golden oar.

Kings I can summon with my hands alone,
And as my fingers through their salt beards combed,
I wept. They sang of victories long gone
And the deep seas their ships had sailed upon.

Clarion calls and deep-voiced shells I hear
That regulate the rhythm of the oar;
The rowers' chanty keeps the rhythm tame,

And gods on the heroic prow up high,
Archaic smiles bespattered by the foam,
Hold out indulgent sculpted arms to me.

Pomegranates

O pomegranates! Seeds
So pack your tough, taut rind
They burst it like a mind
Drunk with discoveries.

The sun that works its will
To bring you to fruition
Softens your hard gold shell
And there begins to spill

Obedient to some power
Bright red through each partition,
Each drop a scarlet jewel.

The wound's illumination
Allows me to envision
Your secret inmost bower.

KONSTANTINE KARYOTAKIS
(1896–1928)

Spirochaeta Pallida

Beautiful, taken all in all, those scientific books
with blood-red illustrations. After several dubious looks
at these, my friend (another beauty) giggled secretly;
and there was beauty too in what her fleeting lips gave me,

which gently yet persistently came tapping at each head.
We opened up so she could march imperiously in,
Mistress Madness. Once inside, she locked the door again.
Since then our life is like a story strange and old and sad.

Logical thought and feeling now are luxuries, excess.
We give them both away for free to any prudent man,
while holding onto childish snickers, wild impulsiveness.
Whatever is instinctive we've committed to God's hand.

Since all of His creation is a horrid comedy,
the author and producer—His intentions are the best—
has rung the curtain down so that we do not have to see
the dazzling performance lost in dimness, dreams, and
mist.

Beautiful, taken all in all, our little purchased friend
that winter twilight long ago when, enigmatically
laughing, she leaned forward for a kiss. And she could see
like a yawning gulf the way it probably would end.

Ode to a Young Child

They all have gone away,
Ari, along with you.
The furniture reverts
to solitude; the gifts
seek little hands that swayed
like lilies on a stalk.

Those days of things first seen
are silent, empty now;
staircases, rooms are still.
And none of us can know
whether your infant gaze
will light on them again.

Pottering about,
I close and open doors
and laugh without a cause
and mutter at the walls
bitter words to wake
echoes still asleep.

The empty jardiniere:
a perfect place for toys!
Atop your little sheep
the monkey straddles—there.
Lastly but not least,
your wide-winged butterfly.

As by a tempest now
the family house is tossed,
shuddering to its foundations
as Time comes marching through.
Suddenly I see
how I'm alone and last.

For all the joys to come
I bless you, little boy,
a smile upon your lips
for a world still unknown,
my guardian angel, light,
and consolation!

Justification

Poetry, farewell! I'm leaving you
to go on humming without me somehow.
People's laughter and the winds that wail
will have to keep you on an even keel.

My plan is to lie down, eyes shut,
and laugh the last and best laugh yet.
"Good night; and give my love to light"
I'll tell the last man that I meet.

When we slowly hit the road
they'll find that I'm a heavy load
(for the first time) on four men's backs.

Taking over my life's strain
finally, shovelfuls will rain
beautifully down upon me: thorns, clods, rocks.

Ideal Suicides

They turn their key in the door,
take letters to read again
in secret one more time,
and stump across the floor.

Tragic, they call their lives.
God! People's awful sneers,
homesickness, sweat, tears,
longing for friendly skies.

They stand at the window to see
nature: a child, a tree,
stonemasons pounding away,
the sun about to set permanently.

It's over. There's the note—
weighty, concise, that's right.
Forgiveness and indifference
await the sad recipient.

They check their watch and the mirror
(is this all a crazy error?);
"It's over—now," they say.
But tomorrow's another day.

Military March

Meander patterns on the ceiling's white
into their plaster dance are drawing me.
The happiness I feel must be
a matter of height.

Symbols of transcendency abound:
a wheel of mystic power,
a white acanthus flower,
and the sculpted horn they both surround.

Humble art without the least pretense,
I learn your lesson late,
dream molded in relief which I can sense
only in terms of height.

Too many boundaries are choking me.
In every clime and latitude,
struggles for one's daily bread,
love affairs, ennui.

But let me now put on
that handsome plaster crown.
Thus bordered by the ceiling I shall be
a splendid sight to see.

Precautions

When people want to hurt you,
they'll always manage to.
Fling down your gun and grovel
when they are passing through.

God help you when you hear
the tramp of wolfish feet.
Lie down flat and hold your breath
and keep your eyes shut tight.

Seek out somewhere in the wide world,
one secret place, one spot.
People with evil in their hearts
know how to dress it up

persuasively with golden words
not one of which is true
since what's at stake is nothing less
than flesh and blood—yes, you.

When you have only your good heart
to keep you company,
go cut yourself a flowering branch
to wear like a bouquet

in your buttonhole. Pimps and whores—
forget them, the whole tribe
as into the grim gulf you fall,
your lyre clutched to your side.

Clerical Workers

Clerical workers flicker and go out
two by two, uninsulated wires.
Twin electricians—Death and the State—
can make repairs.

Clerical workers sit in chairs and blot
innocent white paper needlessly.
"And thus I have the honor, Sir, to be
etc." they write.

That honor's all that's left them when
each night at eight they climb the hill
mechanically, clockwork men,

buy chestnuts, pondering each rule
and regulation of exchange,
and shrug their shoulders: none of this will change.

Invocation

I know that you're approaching, gloomy Night.
Your outstretched claws are groping. By your breath
shrivelled, both flowers and fire meet their death.
And now you cover me, your wings spread wide.

I need a little time still, sovereign Night!
My own desires I promise to suppress
and to assume like a distorted face
what other people seem to feel: delight.

At least that way there will be some excuse
(a tattered banner from a long-lost war),
as that my soul feels something more than sheer
terror (unworthy thought, to be dismissed!).

The image, not the real experience
of suffering, I want to face just once.
And then I'll be all yours. O take me back
and wrap me firmly, Night, in endless black!

Autumn, What Can I Say to You?

Autumn, what can I say to you? Your earliest breath is
drawn
from city lights; you reach as far as heaven's cloudy air.
Hymns, symbols, early drafts of poems, all of them well
known—
the mind's cold blossoms—fall like withered leaves in
your long hair.

Imperious, gigantic apparition, as you walk
along the path of bitterness, of sudden snatchings up,
your lofty forehead strikes the stars; the hem of your gold
cloak
drives dead leaves along the ground with its relentless
sweep.

You are destruction's angel, master of the death you bring,
the shadow which with nightmare pace advances on its
way;
from time to time deliberately you flap a fearful wing,
and sketch unending questions, questions all across the sky.

O autumn, I was full of longing for your chilly weather,
those trees, that forest, even the deserted pedestal;
and as back down to clammy earth both fruit and branches
fall,
I've come, a captive of your passion: let us die
together.

I Am the Garden

I am the garden many a fragrant bloom
filled once, and cheerful twitterings of birds,
where strolling friends could whisper secret words
here in the shadows, where love was at home.

I am the garden still in that same spot.
In vain I wait for someone to return.
Instead of roses now I put forth thorns
that stifle nightingales, where vipers knot.

Posthumous Fame

Limitless nature needs for us to die.
Flower mouths open like a purple cry.
Spring may return—to disappear again;
we shall be less than shades of shadows then.

The brilliant sun is waiting for our death.
One more triumphal sunset we shall see,
and after that from April evenings flee
toward the dark domains that lie beneath.

[If in our lives we suffer the same pain,
or age, frail children in a reverie,
we flee from here without the slightest gain,
not even memories of a wasted day.]

After us nothing but our verse will stay,
a mere ten lines of poetry, the way,
when shipwrecked voyagers fling out doves to fate,
the message they deliver comes too late.

Final Journey

Good voyage on the boundless sea, O disappearing boat!
You sail along embraced by darkness with your golden
light.
If only I were standing on your prow, my circling gaze
Would fix on dreams that pass like a procession of praise.

Oh, on the ocean and in life may every storm grow calm,
And may I, fleeing far with you, toss just one stone behind
me, while you, boat, rock my grief, my grief that has no
end—
not knowing where you're taking me, and never to
return!

How Young

Washed up here on this desert island, young as we still are,
here at the world's end, dreams as far away as solid land!
Having finally lost sight of our remaining friend,
hither we slowly dragged ourselves with our eternal scar.

With empty eyes and halting step we somehow move
  along,
all of us on the same road yet each of us alone;
we sense our sickly body like a sudden alien weight;
our voice sounds far away and hollow as a distant shout.

A siren on the far horizon, life is passing by,
but it will bring us only death and anger day by day,
as long as sunbeams laugh and gentle breezes blow. And we?
Well, here we are, marooned. And we are very young to be

abandoned thus at night, cast up right here upon a rock
by a ship now disappearing in the vast sea's heart;
and as it vanishes we ask what is it we have done
that we are all so fugitive, so quenched, and still so
  young!

The Moon Tonight

The moon upon the sea will fall,
a heavy pearl, tonight,
and frolic all around me like a fool,
that mad moonlight.

A ruby-colored wave will break in foam
at my feet, scattering
stars; and my two hands will have become
doves on the wing

and birdlike will ascend—a silvery pair
of cups now, full of moon,
and sprinkle moonbeams gently down upon
my shoulders and my hair.

The ocean is one liquid golden sheet.
I'll put my dream into a little boat
and let it drift, and crunch the diamond-bright
beach pebbles underfoot.

My heart, that heavy pearl, will shine
through the surrounding glow,
and I shall laugh and wish to weep . . . And oh,
look! The moon!

Preveza

Death is the cranes
that bump into the roofs and the black wall;
death is the local dames
who make love peeling onions all the while.

Death is each shabby street
with its resonant, resplendent name,
the olive grove, the sea below spread out,
and death of all the other deaths, the sun.

Death the policeman who so carefully
wraps up and weighs his "insufficient" dinner,
and death the hyacinths on the balcony,
the teacher, nose forever in his paper.

Ah, Preveza, fortress and garrison!
On Sunday we'll go listen to the band.
I got a savings booklet from the bank.
First deposit: thirty drachmas down.

Strolling slowly up and down the quay,
"Do I exist?" you say. "You're not alive!"
Here comes the steamer, and her flag flies high.
His Excellency the Governor may arrive.

If at least one person from this place
from horror, boredom, and disgust would drop,
silent and solemn, each with a long face,
at the funeral we'd all live it up.